HOW TO DEVELOP YOUR CHILD'S GIFTS AND TALENTS IN MATH

D1570207

HOW TO DEVELOP YOUR CHILD'S GIFTS AND TALENTS IN MATH

by
Ronn Yablun

Lowell House
Los Angeles

Contemporary Books
Chicago

Library of Congress Cataloging-in-Publication Data

Yablun, Ronn.
     How to develop your child's gifts and talents in math / by Ronn Yablun.
        p. cm.
     ISBN 1-56565-338-6
     1. Mathematics—Study and teaching (Elementary) 2. Mathematical
ability. 3. Education, Elementary—Parent participation.
I. Title.
QA135.5.Y3   1995
649'.68—dc20   95-35244
                                                                      CIP

Requests for such permissions should be addressed to:
Lowell House
2029 Century Park East, Suite 3290
Los Angeles, CA 90067

Lowell House books can be purchased at special discounts when
ordered in bulk for premiums and special sales. Contact Department JH at the
address above.

Publisher: Jack Artenstein
General Manager, Lowell House Adult: Bud Sperry
Managing Editor: Maria Magallanes
Text Design: Laurie Young

Manufactured in the United States of America
10 9 8 7 6 5 4 3 2 1

CONTENTS

APPENDICES

ACKNOWLEDGMENTS

Special thanks to Karen Boras for her invaluable ideas and assistance; Beth Matustik for her constant support and inspiration; Gloria Patterson for her grammatical genius; Sharon Wheeler for her invaluable advice; Michael for helping me keep my sanity; Mom and Dad for always being there; to my fearless editor, Bud; special thanks to my exceptional kid Dale; and to all my students, past and present, who continue to teach me more than I could ever teach them.

I dedicate this book to my three children,
Melissa, Alex, and Mark.

INTRODUCTION

A Word to Parents

Teaching your child math can be an extraordinary experience. Opening a child's eyes to the magic of numbers can be rewarding in a way that only a parent and/or a teacher can truly understand. However, as exhilarating as the experience can be, it can also be demanding since we, as parents, have certain expectations of our own children that no others would ever dream of imposing on them. Often times we have a limited window of patience with our own children, and I have found this is due to unreasonably high expectations. Maybe we think our own children should learn faster and more readily than everyone else's children.

The key to this entire dialogue is patience. It cannot be emphasized enough when success is the ultimate goal of the academic program. If you find your patience waning, it's best to end the program for the day and begin fresh the next day. It will keep your position intact and save you the headaches and frustration you are sure to encounter if you continue past your teaching threshold.

The best you can do for your child is to keep the atmosphere light and nonthreatening.

If you encounter a skill your child cannot seem to comprehend, try another technique, try another strategy, or just wait for another day. You'd be amazed how quickly a child can sense a change in attitude and how quickly he or she can turn off and tune out a situation when the positive has suddenly become negative. Imagine yourself in a hostile environment during an argument and you may begin to imagine the way a child feels when a positive climate becomes negative. The key to teaching is simple: The more positive the climate remains during instruction, the more receptive a child is to new ideas.

It is very important to break up learning into blocks of time. Youngsters ordinarily have short attention spans so you will want to break up the lessons and combine pencil/paper activities with more active learning to keep their interest and keep them motivated. It is also important to integrate their learning into their everyday lives so they make realistic connections between academic concepts and the real world.

As a classroom teacher, I often find myself taking things for granted with my students. It is rather easy to do, but I also find it extremely important to stay focused on what I am really trying to accomplish with my students. Occasionally I will notice a student "drifting away" in class and it's at those particular moments that I am reminded of what my job is truly all about. Like most teachers, I often call on the student who does not appear to be paying attention in class. This is not done as a punitive measure, but rather as a means of drawing that student back into the discussion. I, myself, remember daydreaming as a child (Don't we all?), yet the harsh reality of it is that we do need to stay focused to accomplish. The challenge I face on a daily basis is that of trying to "entertain" thirty-five students all at once. You, on the other hand, have a captive audience of one. Take advantage of that. Capitalize on it. Have fun with it.

Throughout this book you are provided with ideas for making these connections in meaningful ways. Hopefully, as you progress with your child, you will find your own creative solutions that your child will come to truly understand and appreciate. Just remember to keep it light, nonthreatening, and, most of all, fun.

Getting Familiar with Numbers

E verywhere you look, there are numbers. On street signs, in advertisements, in newspapers, in your car, in your home . . . there is no escaping them. We need to understand them so that we can use them to our advantage, but to do this we must master them. Children need to be exposed to numbers in every way, shape, and form to begin to feel comfortable using them. But first, they need to understand the unique characteristics that numbers possess. This chapter is designed to help you help your child understand some of these characteristics and how these characteristics affect numbers and how numbers affect them.

Numbers are truly magical in that they have very unique characteristics. Each number has characteristics that most other numbers do not. For example, the number one is the only whole number that divides evenly into all other whole numbers. The number two is the only number, other than one, that divides evenly into all even whole numbers. Counting by threes, fours, and so on will yield a variety of answers that will, in fact, prove that numbers each have their own truly unique characteristics.

When discussing number recognition, it is important to help children understand that numbers can be found on street signs, in the grocery store, in your car, on television and, most everywhere you look, numbers play *some* role in every part of everyday living. Bringing these numbers to life is very important to a child's awareness of his or her surroundings, and for that reason the power of numbers and mathematics should never be underestimated.

When you begin discussing numbers with your child, you might want to keep a journal with your child to keep track of how numbers are used and what they are used for. This simple exercise will help your child understand the importance of numbers in their lives.

A good exercise to begin with might be to just walk around the house with your child and let your child find every item possible that either has numbers on it or uses numbers. Use this opportunity to identify the numbers individually and explain the difference in their values to your child. Even you will be amazed with the number of items you will encounter. This is the perfect opportunity to start bringing math to life for your child.

You might even want to have your child try to keep track of the many places numbers appear when you are in your car en route from home to the supermarket or to the post office (which in itself is an amazing mathematical entity). Simple exercises like these are most certainly opportunities to arouse a child's curiosity about numbers and mathematics.

The more attention you give to the numbers around you, the more likely your child will develop an interest in learning more about numbers and their uses.

SOME BEGINNING EXERCISES

Here are some simple exercises to bring attention to numbers for your child.

When taking a short trip in your car, have your child identify every number that he or she sees that has a five in it. Keep track of these and perhaps on the return trip have your child identify every number that he or she sees that has a zero in it. Comparing these results is a follow-up activity that could provide an interesting discussion between you and your child. You could discuss which numbers are more popular, which are less popular, and perhaps why your child might think one number is more popular than another. Of course this will involve preliminary work on your part in terms of writing for and with your child the digits five and zero. You might even want to provide alternatives. For example, if there are two children in the car, assign each child a different number to see who can recognize and identify the most possibilities during your trip. The possibilities in this exercise are endless.

If you are cabinbound, another fun activity is to take a desk drawer and ask your child to find as many items in this particular drawer as he or she can with numbers on them. You could also limit this exercise to a particular number if you wanted to make the activity more challenging. However, you will probably want to supervise this activity closely . . . or you could wind up with a major mess on your hands!

Perhaps a trip to the supermarket could provide an opportunity for your child to explore further the characteristics of numbers. Your child could look to see how many different numbers there are. He or she could also look to see how many items have the same price listed. You might want to use this opportunity to explain to your child how numbers are used in the supermarket and how each number represents a different price and what the prices are based on. You could spend some time explaining why some items are more expensive than others and what it means to be "expensive" as opposed to "reasonable." The possibilities in the supermarket are endless.

A trip to the post office exposes your child to stamps, their costs, and their uses. Every branch of the post office has a booklet about stamp collecting that you could use to discuss with your child the value of stamps, past and present.

There are other activities that don't involve money that also utilize numbers and increase your child's understanding of the many uses of numbers. For example, speed limit signs, telephones, clocks, microwave ovens, addresses, sports scores, calendars, thermometers, television stations, and even clothing sizes are a few of the other ways children begin to see and use numbers.

Perhaps at this point you might want to sit and make a list with your child of the many places numbers can be found. This list could be used as a lead into a discussion with your child of the many uses of numbers in people's everyday lives. By this point, you most certainly will have aroused your child's curiosity about numbers!

Remember, however, there is a most definite sequence to learning mathematics. To begin, your child should learn to count. Counting initiates the sequence of learning numbers so your child can more fully understand their characteristics and their usage.

LEARNING TO COUNT

Once your child has become comfortable with the basic characteristics of numbers and number recognition, you can begin exploring the possibilities of counting. Your child's knowledge of sequences will be put to the test in most every math skill he or she attempts. It is fair to say that counting is the springboard to all other math skills, both computational and conceptual.

Teaching your child to count to ten is the first step since this is the most basic of sequences to learn. Eventually you will want to expand on that, but initially one through ten is enough. The numbers from one to ten are formally known as the basic counting numbers. There are a variety of ways you can teach your child to count to ten. One of the easiest ways to remember anything is to set it to music. If you can sing it, you will always remember it.

The first of the most basic songs is, "Ten Little Indians":

One little, two little, three little Indians,
four little, five little, six little Indians,
seven little, eight little, nine little Indians,
ten little Indian boys.

To help your child learn the first ten counting numbers in reverse order the song can be sung in reverse:

Ten little, nine little, eight little Indians,
seven little, six little, five little Indians,
four little, three little, two little Indians,
one little Indian boy.

A rhyme that will help your child learn how to count to ten is "One Two, Buckle My Shoe":

One, two buckle my shoe,
three, four, shut the door
five, six, pick up sticks,

seven, eight, close the gate,
nine, ten, start again!

Another way to help your child learn to count is to count a certain item while you are in the car. For example, have your child count the number of stop signs on the road. Or have your child count the number of traffic signals. Or the number of station wagons. You will help your child remember the order numbers have by constant practice in counting.

Perhaps you could go for a walk and ask your child to count the number of mailboxes or streetlights on your street. Again, use your imagination to create situations that will stimulate your child's abilities and interests. The more practice your child has counting, the more likely he or she is to remember the sequence of numbers. Again, this cannot be emphasized enough!

It is important to integrate counting into your child's daily math routine. It serves as a great opening exercise for most any other skill you plan to focus on for the day.

Below is a list of items you could have your child count as a math warm-up, both inside and outside the house:

1. **Teaspoons**
2. **Coins**
3. **Streetlights**
4. **Cassette tapes**
5. **Stairs**
6. **Steps from one room to another**
7. **Flowering plants**
8. **Automobiles**
9. **Cracks in the sidewalk**
10. **Numbers on the face of a clock**

At this point you might want to expand the counting pattern to include eleven through twenty. Once you feel your child is comfortable with one through ten, the next step is logical. Counting up to twenty increases your child's confidence in that he or she is likely to feel accomplishment in being able to move on, with your help of course. Use your imagination to allow your child to count items that exceed ten, such as books, tapes, and crayons.

Now that your child has mastered counting, it's time to take that skill and provide order to it. Now that your child can count, it's logical to move into patterns and sequences. Counting from one through ten is the most basic sequence; let's take a look beyond that.

PATTERNS AND SEQUENCES

Patterns and sequences are the most significant of mathematical skills. A child's visual perception of objects is important in terms of how he or she perceives numbers and the relationships between numbers. It can also have a profound affect on a child's comprehension of geometry, as this forms the preliminary understanding of objects and how they relate to each other.

A fundamental concept in the area of patterns involves a child's ability to comprehend a pattern and determine what would happen next if the pattern were to continue. Understanding your child's ability to think critically will also help you determine if your child needs to spend more time developing this aspect of his or her learning ability. Let's take a look at a very basic pattern and try to understand conceptually how critical thinking applies.

The pattern on the following page is a fairly simple one. Take a look at it and see if you can determine what shape would be the next if the pattern were to continue:

You should be able to see that the next item in the pattern would be another circle larger than the one before it. The pattern should look like this:

Now that you have the idea, ask your child to attempt the next pattern. Explain to your child that you are going to show him or her a group of shapes. You want your child to look carefully at the pattern and see if he or she can draw for you "what comes next."

Notice that the box keeps getting longer and longer. You may want to discuss what you are seeing, and assist your child in arriving at the answer. This concept is called spatial relationships—how objects relate to each other and the space around them. Then ask your child to draw what comes next.

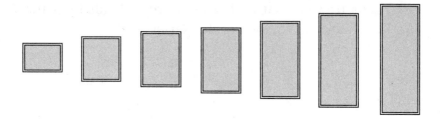

The last rectangle in this drawing is what your child should draw as a representation in the pattern of what comes next. If your child comes out with a different illustration, discuss the answer with your child, being sure to explain what is happening from one picture to the next and what your child should have seen and done to solve the problem. Assure your child that it is not necessary to always get the correct answer. Let's try another one and see how your child performs. Show this pattern to your child and see what responses he or she comes up with in response to the question "What comes next?"

Now ask your child to once again draw a picture of the shape he or she thinks would come next in this illustration. It is quite appropriate to discuss with your child exactly what is happening from one picture to the next before he or she draws the picture. Then tell your child that the picture should look like this:

Let's try one that is slightly more difficult than the previous ones. Take a look at this series:

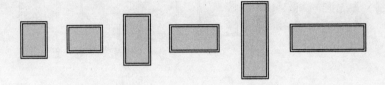

Notice that in addition to the size changing from picture to picture, the position of the shape is also changing. This added dimension makes it somewhat more difficult to solve from a child's perspective. Explain to your child that sometimes in patterns the size *and* the position of the shape can change at the same time. Show your child exactly what is happening in the above illustration, then perhaps he or she will be able to determine what comes next. Don't worry about giving away too much information! You may even want to devise some of your own patterns for your child to attempt:

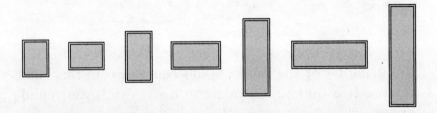

Take a look at Appendix A. On this page there are several different shapes provided for you to reproduce. It is best to make four of each shape and size. You may want to photocopy and enlarge these shapes to make it easier for you to manipulate. Mounting them on cardboard to reinforce them enables you to use them longer. This would also be a good time to sit down with your child and color them together, discussing patterns and how they work. The idea behind reproducing four of each shape and size is to allow you the freedom to experiment with patterns on your own and discuss what you are doing with your child at the time you are doing it.

Here is an example of how to use the shapes in Appendix A to explore the concept of patterns and sequences. After you have colored and cut out the shapes, lay the circles and squares next to each other like this:

Next, ask your child to decide what shape and size comes next. If your child is correct he or she should select the same size circle as the first and second circle in the sequence. If your child chooses something other than this, show him or her the correct shape and explain why his or her answer was not the right choice.

Here is another example of a sequence that is a little more difficult. See if your child can determine the next shape and size in the sequence:

If your child has difficulty determining the next shape and size in the sequence, don't worry. This one is rather difficult compared to the first one since it displays a difference in shape *and* size at the same time. This might confuse some children. The correct answer is a circle larger than the second circle. If you were to go beyond that, the next answer would be a circle larger than the first square. If your child answers incorrectly, explain that the shape and size is changing at the same time and then show him or her which shape and size comes next. This will help your child understand that it is possible for more than one change to be taking place at the same time.

Here is one more example for you to try with your child:

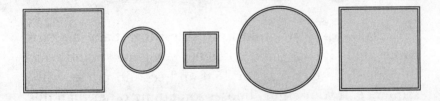

This one is more difficult in that there doesn't seem to be any particular sequence. Upon closer examination, however, you see that there is a very distinct pattern. The sequence of the shapes is square, circle, square, circle, and so on. The sequence of the sizes is large, small, small, large, large . . . so the next shape would be a small circle.

Another way to work with your child on patterns and sequences is to use a simple deck of cards. You can use cards to help your child learn sequences. For example, lay out the two of hearts, the three of hearts, and then the four of hearts. Hand your child the rest of the deck or lay out the rest of the deck on the table. Ask your child to find the card that comes next. Your child should be able to choose the five of hearts. It is not only important your child find the correct number, but also the correct suit.

Try this one with your cards. Lay out the six of hearts,

the six of diamonds, and the six of clubs. Then ask your child to find the other remaining card in the grouping. This might be a little more difficult, but hopefully your child will see that there is another six missing from the group.

You might also want to try this kind of problem. Lay out the ten of hearts, the nine of diamonds, and the eight of clubs. Now, when you ask your child What comes next? you are not only asking what number is next sequentially, but also which suit is part of the pattern. These types of problems can be a little more difficult, but your child is sure to catch on if you persist.

Another way to work with your child on patterns and sequences is to use a set of dominoes. Since each domino has a maximum number of six, you can have fun using patterns with combinations up to six for this activity. For example, lay out dominoes, end to end, in this order: 1/2, 2/3, 3/4, and 4/5. Then ask your child to find the domino that completes the sequence. Hopefully he or she will select the domino 5/6 and place that at the end of the row. You could also try: 1/1, 2/2, 3/3, and ask your child What comes next? The obvious choice is 4/4, but the possibilities you can utilize are endless. This is just another way of making learning a fun experience. A game of dominoes would actually help you work with your child on number recognition skills and basic counting skills. It's also just plain fun.

Another fun activity that you could use for learning patterns and sequences would involve a piece of string and any type of circular cereal with a hole in the middle. Have your child string them together to make a necklace, paying particular attention to the color patterns you select as he or she places them on the string. The completed necklace is fun to wear and/or eat when the activity is complete. You could either establish the initial pattern yourself or have your child select the pattern by choosing the first six or eight items to be strung and then asking him or her to adhere to the same pattern for the rest of the project. This is definitely a fun activity!

For this activity you could also use colored (dyed) macaroni in the same fashion to make a necklace or bracelet. Remember, though, not to consume the end product!

Now that your child has mastered patterns and sequences, learning to measure is the next step in understanding the basic characteristics of numbers. Because your child understands basically what numbers are, he or she can begin to understand how to use them. Learning to measure will be your child's first application skill in mathematics.

LEARNING TO MEASURE

Measuring is the most basic application skill in mathematics. It provides your child with an opportunity to "use" numbers, to provide a basic understanding of how numbers can and should be used for practical purposes. Measuring is also one of the most basic hands-on skills, in that it provides the opportunity for your child to use manipulative devices such as a ruler to physically "do" math. The easiest examples to explain to your child would have to do with carpeting your house or putting new linoleum on the kitchen floor. Measuring is one way of "figuring it out."

To begin these exercises, you will need several items that you will probably be able to find lying around the house. First, you will need a simple twelve-inch ruler. A standard tape measure is helpful if you have one, since this can be used for larger measures. A yardstick could be used if you do not have a tape measure, however the flexibility of the tape measure makes it more desirable for children. Scissors and a ball of twine (actually, kite string is terrific to work with!) can also be used for measuring. Yarn can be used in place of string if you like.

First, you will need to sit down with your child and explain the basic units of measure. Most importantly, you will need to show and discuss the inch mark and the foot mark on the ruler. Let your child actually count the number of inches in one foot by using the numbers from one to twelve on the ruler. Show your child the other side of the ruler where metric measure is used. For our purposes, we won't be using the metric portion of the ruler, but you may want to show your child so he or she knows which side of the ruler to refer to when we are discussing inches and feet.

While measuring items, we are going to be doing a great deal of estimating. Rarely is the case when we measure an item that it will measure exactly three inches or exactly one foot. Most likely, an item will measure $3\frac{1}{8}$ inches or $1\frac{1}{3}$ feet. So, what you'll need to address first is the skill of estimating or rounding off. The easiest way to address this topic is to look at a ruler and ask your child which one-inch marking the item is "closer" to. This will help your child "estimate" his or her answers.

For hands-on experience, you will probably want to set this exercise up before your child joins you. Select about five or six items to be measured that are less than one foot. This way, you can use a twelve-inch ruler for the exercise. You want to be sure *not* to use breakable items or items that have sharp corners or edges since your child will be handling these items. The following items are examples that you might want to consider using:

1. A teaspoon
2. A paperback book
3. A pen or pencil
4. A photograph
5. An envelope

Once you have completed this exercise, you might want to design a scavenger hunt for your child (within the house) that will involve your child first finding items you designate and then measuring the items one at a time.

As an example, I would compile a list of five not-so-hard-to-find items and give your child ten minutes to complete the task. Ask him or her to first find the items and bring them to the kitchen table. Once they are on the table, ask your child to measure each of the items. This will make it more of a game and less of a chore.

Next, you might want to move this exercise outdoors. You could also incorporate the "scavenger hunt" idea outside to maximize the game aspect of this exercise. Easy-to-measure outdoor items include a leaf, the height of a stair, a planter box, and a birdhouse. Be careful to select items that are flat and safe to measure. If you are going to conduct a scavenger hunt, make sure you are including items such as leaves, twigs, and small stones. Just remember that estimating is the key to this exercise.

Next you might want your child to measure certain parts of his or her body, such as the length of the foot, the width of the palm, or even the length of one finger. You can use a tape measure to measure your child's height or waist size.

You should not limit your measuring activities to linear (straight line) measures. You can also incorporate activities that include liquid measure. For example, you might want to see how many teaspoons or tablespoons of sugar are needed to make one-quarter of a cup. Or perhaps you might want to see how many cups of water it takes to make one quart. Involving your child in these activities will help your child see that measurement is not only limited to the use of a tape measure.

A fun way to involve your child in an active learning activity is to make a box recipe of cupcakes or brownies. As part of the directions, have your child assist in measuring the necessary ingredients for the mixture. Allow your child to pour the necessary ingredients into your batter so he or she sees that it is important for every item to be measured exactly. You might even want to explain to your child what might happen if the ingredients are not measured accurately. You might want to ask your child how the finished product would taste if there were too much sugar or too little butter. It might even be interesting to experiment this way and actually prepare a recipe with intentionally wrong amounts to see what the true end result tastes like!

Later on in life your child will probably be exposed to metric measurement as well, but I would hesitate to make an issue of it at this point since it far exceeds anything you are likely to encounter at this stage in your child's development.

However, understanding the basic concepts and skills of liquid and solid measures is an integral part of each and every child's basic math initiation. Measurements are used in practical settings with life experiences and can affect how a child selects a right or a wrong pair of shoes or even a right or a wrong shirt. Your child's own math experiences will shape his or her true perceptions of his or her own world. The activities associated with basic measuring can, in fact, turn out to be a great deal of fun! It all depends on how you approach your subject.

SHAPES AND SIZES

In the exploration of shapes and sizes, recognition of similar shapes cannot be underestimated. Knowledge of similar shapes (with both the same and different sizes) introduces a child to the study of geometry. Geometry, as defined by *Webster's*, is "a branch of mathematics that deals with the measurement, properties, and relationships of points, lines, angles, surfaces, and solids." Basically, we are talking about the relationships of shapes and sizes.

It is very easy to make the study of shapes and sizes a game and, no doubt, something your child is likely to enjoy. As a simple example, take a look at the shapes below:

If you were to ask your child which of the objects is different, he or she would most likely select the last one. This, however, is a basic example of how the differences of shapes become less easily recognizable and the level of difficulty increases dramatically. Perhaps it would be a good idea to also discuss the names given to each of the shapes, the oval or ellipse and the rectangle, and the characteristics of each shape. These names are used in geometry and it is certainly helpful to acclimate your child to the names of the various geometric shapes.

As an example of a more difficult pattern recognition problem, take a look at the one below.

You have to look very carefully to see the difference in the shapes. The difference is not easily recognizable, but if you look closely, you will see that the second shape from the left is slightly different than the others. Notice that the upper right hand corner of the shape is slightly lower compared to the same side of the other shapes. So you see that there are easier and more complex situations involving shapes that might make this experience a little more difficult for your child to grasp. Again, the key is patience . . . you can always come back to it another day.

Now, let's try a simple exercise with your child to see if he or she can differentiate between different shapes. Ask your child to look at the rows of shapes on the next page and tell which shape does not belong in each row. The first one is somewhat obvious, but notice that the level of difficulty increases with each problem:

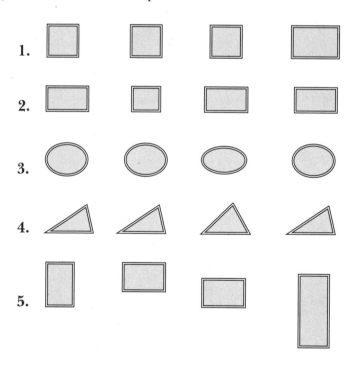

It's a good idea to always begin with the easier, more obvious patterns before progressing to the more complex ones. This allows your child to experience immediate success and thereby motivate your child to continue. Here is another set you can try, with one major change. Notice that the positioning of the figures is changing, which adds complexity to the selection process.

Ask your child to select the one object that is different in each row:

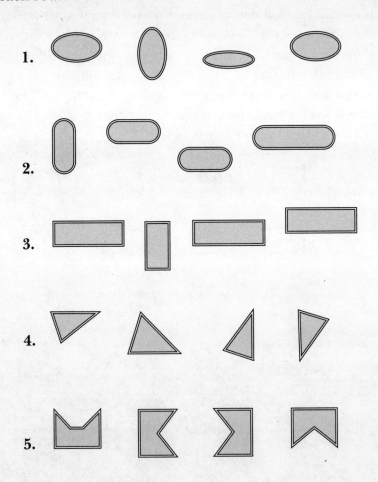

Now that you have the idea, let's explore the issue of size. Although objects may have the same shape, if their size varies the characteristics of the object change. Look at the items below and ask your child to identify the shape that does not belong. In other words, objects of the same shape may be related even if their sizes vary:

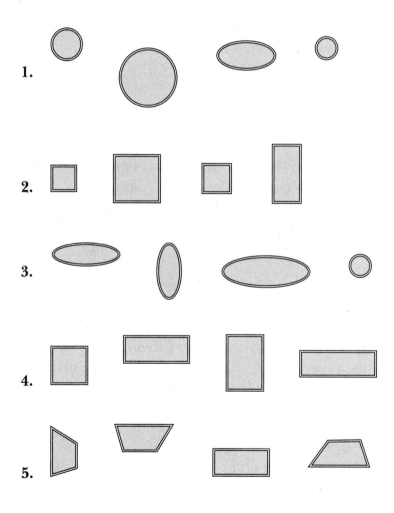

Now let's try the same type of situation in a less visual format. Ask your child which object does not belong in each set. You might want to read the objects out loud to your child if your child has not yet mastered reading words. Feel free to provide definitions and even examples of each so your child clearly understands the meaning of each object. See if your child can differentiate between the items in each set. You will probably want to entertain a discussion of each problem to help your child fully understand why items do and do not belong together. Your child needs to understand how groupings work and how objects relate to each other. You will want to emphasize that the groupings are based on shapes *and* sizes.

Which object does *not* belong in the set?

1. circle   oval   square   ellipse
2. rectangle   oval   square   triangle
3. orange   banana   apple   tangerine
4. doughnut   bagel   pancake   sandwich
5. baseball   book   envelope   magazine

At this point, a trip to the park might be a great idea. This allows you to discuss the differences between different leaves and flowers and even trees and what makes them similar and what makes them different. You should discuss with your child that it is not only shape and size that make objects both similar and different. Taking two or even three leaves from a tree will allow you to explore the differences and similarities between the leaves, even though they come from the same tree. You might even want to ask your child if he or she can think of other similar objects that can be different in both shape and size.

A simple experiment with two identical balloons can help your child understand the most basic concepts of "same and different." Inflate two balloons to two different sizes. Ask your child how they are the same. He or she should include as part of the answer the fact that they are the same color and the same shape. When you ask your child how they are different, he or she should respond that they are different sizes. Less noticeable differences include color, in that, ordinarily, the more inflated a balloon becomes, the less of the initial color it retains. If you want to get technical, when two identical balloons are inflated with different amounts of air, the chances are pretty good that the two balloons will have completely different sizes. Most children would never expect this to happen, although it does depend entirely on the elasticity of the balloon itself. And although these are technical points, discussing them is helpful to avoid confusion over similarities and differences.

In conclusion, any discussion of shapes and sizes needs to include exploration with everyday objects that children can relate to. The more of the real world you involve in your discussion, the more the child will be able to relate his or her own world to his or her learning experiences. We can never underestimate the value of learning concretely at an early age, since most young children have a great deal of difficulty understanding and grasping abstract concepts. Once they completely comprehend concrete, basic concepts, then the abstract can be used to explore further possibilities and relationships. However, children will always use their previous knowledge to explore and understand even the most basic of abstract concepts.

Hopefully at this point your child has a better understanding of numbers, what they are, and how they can be used. The next step we are going to take involves operating with numbers. Now that your child understands what numbers *are*, we want to show your child what numbers *do*.

Learning to Add and Subract

Basic addition and subtraction are skills that require a child's complete comprehension of the basic characteristics of numbers. Be certain that your child fully understands chapter 1 before embarking on the basic operations of addition and subtraction. The more fully aware your child is of the characteristics of numbers, the more likely he or she is to succeed with basic operations.

To begin, you will need to refer to Appendix B. The operational counting sticks in the appendix are used as a manipulative device to help your child "see" how the operations with numbers work. Making the operations concrete provides the explanation at the same time as providing the solution. Follow the directions on page 135 for creating your own set of counting sticks. Again you may want to photocopy and enlarge these to make it easier for your child to manipulate. You will need to have two of each size to begin working with addition and subtraction. Using a cardboard-like material will increase durability. The kitchen table is a great place to work with your child on cutting and coloring these counting sticks. For your information, you will need to know the values of each of the sticks (listed in Appendix B), so marking the value with a permanent black marker before your child begins to color them will help with the identification process.

Once the coloring sticks have been cut out, numbered, and colored, spread them out on the table. First explain to your child that you are going to demonstrate how to add or total two numbers together. Give your child a concrete example that will help him or her understand the concept of adding two numbers together. For example, "Mommy has five sweaters and Daddy has four sweaters. How many sweaters do they have altogether?" Take a silver counting stick (which represents 5) and a yellow counting stick (which represents 4) and lay them end to end on the table. Explain that the silver counting stick (5) is the number of Mommy's sweaters and the yellow counting stick (4) is the number of Daddy's sweaters.

Lay the yellow and silver counting sticks end to end. Then, ask your child to find a counting stick that is just as long as the silver and yellow counting sticks together, and lay it next to them. The only counting stick that is the same length as the silver and yellow together is the gold (9) counting stick. Once your child has found this counting stick and placed it beside the other two, ask him or her what number is on the counting stick he or she selected. Your child should respond with nine. Then tell your child that this is the answer you get when you add five and four. Also, constantly remind your child that what you are doing is "adding the silver and the yellow counting sticks together." You can even have your child count five items of one kind and then four items of another kind and finally count them altogether to reinforce the answer. This should help your child see that the counting sticks are an easier way to provide him or her with accurate answers.

Next try this problem. "Mommy has three pencils in her purse. Mommy also has five pencils in the desk drawer. How many pencils does Mommy have altogether?" Ask your child to find the counting stick with the number 3 (pink) on it. Tell your child that this is the number of pencils Mommy has in her purse. Next, ask your child to find the counting stick with the number 5 (silver) on it. Tell your child that this is the number of pencils Mommy has in the desk drawer.

Ask your child to lay the counting sticks end to end. Now ask your child to find the counting stick that is just as long as the pink and the silver counting sticks are together. Your child should, after testing several of them, find the black (8) counting stick is the exact same length. Now ask your child what number is on the black counting stick. When your child answers eight, tell him or her that this is the answer you get when you add three and five.

Remind your child that this process is called addition, or adding. Tell your child that adding two or more items together will always result in a total or sum. These are key words your child will need to know in addition. It is extremely beneficial to keep reminding your child of the key words and their meanings as they relate to addition. Use the key words often in your conversation with your child to help reinforce the words and their meanings. The more reinforcement on the subject, the more likely he or she is to remember.

Let's try one more problem. "Daddy has four tires on his car. He has one more tire in his trunk. How many tires does he have altogether?" Ask your child to find the counting stick with the number 4 (yellow) on it. Tell your child that this is the number of tires on Daddy's car. Next, ask your child to find the counting stick with the number 1 (brown) on it. Tell your child that this is the tire in Daddy's trunk.

Ask your child to lay the counting sticks end to end. Now ask him or her to find the counting stick that is just as long as the yellow and the brown ones are together. Your child should, after testing several of them, find the silver counting stick will be the same length. Now, ask him or her what number is on the silver counting stick. When he or she answers five, tell him or her that this is the answer you get when you add four and one. You might even at this point introduce the plus sign (+). Explain that this is the symbol that is used in addition. It means to add two or more numbers together.

You might also want to get away from the problem-solving strategies to see if your child is truly understanding the concept of addition. Try these problems with your child without any situation to relate it to. If you feel more comfortable making "real-life" problems, then feel free to continue using that approach. You will, however, need to eventually steer away from these real-life problems to see that your child is truly grasping the concept of addition. Ask him or her to add the following problems, one at a time, and then discuss each answer before you proceed to the next one:

1. 4 + 2
2. 3 + 1
3. 2 + 2
4. 5 + 3
5. 1 + 6

Another way to teach your child to add is to use small coinlike or oblong candies, such as jellybeans. Use a small bag to begin. Open up the bag on the table and ask your child to separate the jellybeans by color. Place each color in a separate bowl. Once this task is complete you are ready to begin teaching addition. Ask your child to count out five candies from the red bowl and place them on the table in front of him or her. Next, ask your child to count out four candies from the brown bowl and place those next to the red ones already in front of him or her. Finally, ask your child to count them altogether. If your child counts correctly, the answer should be nine. You can select numerous different combinations to continue with this exercise. Your child will find it's a fun way to play with candy. When finished with this exercise, you might want to reward your child by letting him or her eat a certain number of each of the colors. Or you might want to allow your child to eat the ones that he or she gets correct when doing an addition problem. Having your child count them again before he or she eats them will help reinforce counting skills. You might even want to use the operational counting sticks as part of the exercise with the jellybeans. For example, have your child count out three of one color and four of another color and lay them out on the table. Ask your child to count them altogether. He or she should get seven as his or her answer. Now to reinforce the answer, ask your child to use the pink and yellow counting sticks to arrive at their sum. Your child will also find the answer to be the same, seven. This should help reinforce addition skills.

Another way to help teach addition involves nothing more than a pair of dice. Using a pencil and a pad of paper, ask your child to roll the dice and write down the numbers that appear on each face of the die. Then ask your child to add the two numbers together to get a total for the pair of dice. Your child will rely on his or her counting ability to achieve this task. Continue this rolling of the dice for five throws and then help your child tally the first five rolls. You can continue this game as long as you need to get the point across. This should actually be the point where your child starts transferring the skill of addition to pencil and paper. Remember, it is important that your child utilize pencil and paper for adding, since this is a commonplace activity in the school environment. The earlier your child can adapt to this, the more likely he or she is to succeed in addition. Combining manipulatives with pencil to paper activities alleviates boredom through repetition and helps children feel more successful in a variety of formats. It's appropriate to use the operational counting sticks with the dice to reinforce the addition process.

After using a variety of approaches, you might want to introduce a basic calculator to your instructional strategy. Once a child thoroughly understands the concept of addition, a calculator can be used to show your child that technology has created a way to expedite simple mathematical processes. Go through the necessary key strokes, step by step, with your child to demonstrate how it actually works. You will probably also notice that your child will feel like a grown-up using a calculator, since this is what most adults use. This type of positive reinforcement is very instrumental in children's successes in math. One important point to keep in mind: Do not let your child use *only* a calculator to solve addition problems. Fostering that type of dependency only inhibits a child's ability to grow and understand the mechanics of the process. Occasional use is all that is recommended. Make the calculator a friendly, fun companion to your child, however, insist that your child use his or her own abilities and skills to solve problems. I often explain to my students that they will need to use their "built-in" calculator to solve problems. If the day should arise that a student's electronic calculator breaks or gets lost, then that student is going to need to depend on his or her own abilities to solve problems.

At this point you should begin to see that the boundaries for teaching addition are endless. You could incorporate plastic straws, plastic spoons, macaroni, and numerous other household items to assist you in teaching your child how to add.

Now that we have covered addition, let's take a look at subtraction. You might want to mention to your child that what you are going to do next is the opposite of addition. Instead of putting things together to get a total, you will now be taking things away from the total. Using the words "take away" is the easiest way for you to convey—and your child to understand—the concept of subtraction.

Teaching your child subtraction is very similar to teaching addition. To teach your child subtraction, you can use basically the same items we used to teach addition, since the processes are mere opposites. Let's begin with the operational counting sticks.

Ask your child to spread out the counting sticks on the table with the color side facing up. You are then ready to begin the teaching of this concept. To begin, try this problem: "Mommy had three cartons of milk in the refrigerator. Yesterday, Daddy finished one of the cartons. How many cartons are left?" Ask your child to find the counting stick with the number 3 (pink) on it. Say that this is the number of milk cartons that were in the refrigerator to begin with. Next, ask your child to find the counting stick with the number 1 (brown) on it. Say that is the number of milk cartons that Daddy finished.

Next, ask your child to lay the short counting stick next to the long counting stick, lining them up at one end. Now, your child needs to find the counting stick that he or she can add to the short counting stick to make it as long as the longer counting stick. When the counting sticks are laid side by side their lengths should be exactly the same. After several tries, your child should select the blue (2) counting stick. Finally, explain that the blue counting stick represents the number of milk cartons that are left in the refrigerator.

Let's try another problem. "Daddy had nine suits in his closet. He took three of them to the dry cleaners. How many should be in the closet now?" Ask your child to find the counting stick with the number 9 (gold) on it. Say that this is the number of suits Daddy had in the closet. Now ask your child to find the counting stick with the number 3 (pink) on it. Say that this is the number of suits Daddy took to the dry cleaners.

Next, ask your child to lay the counting sticks side by side, lining them up at one end. Now he or she needs to find the counting stick that, when added on to the short counting stick, becomes the same length as the longer counting stick. When laid side by side, the sticks should be the same length. After several tries, your child should select the orange counting stick (6). Finally, explain that the orange counting stick represents the number of suits Daddy has in the closet.

You can make up problems of your own to use. Make them as relevant to your own situation as possible. Most children will be excited about doing problems that have to do with them or their immediate families. Most of all, make them fun.

At this point, you might want to try several subtraction problems without real-life situations to see if your child thoroughly understands the concept of subtraction. Again, you should feel free to use real-life situations as long as you deem necessary. However, you will need to eventually wean your child from these so that you can be sure he or she thoroughly understands the concept of subtraction. Try these problems, one at a time, taking the time to discuss the answers with your child:

1. $8 - 3$
2. $4 - 2$
3. $9 - 4$
4. $3 - 1$
5. $5 - 5$

You can also use jellybeans in a similar fashion. On your kitchen table, open a bag of these and ask your child to separate them by color and place each color in an individual bowl.

Select a particular color and ask your child to count all of the candies in that bowl. It is best to keep the total at a maximum of twenty candies. From that bowl, after your child has counted them, ask him or her to take a handful of the candies and place them on the table. Next, ask your child to count the candies on the table. Explain to your child that when you "take away" the candies from the bowl, you are subtracting them from the original total.

Now let your child count the number of candies left in the bowl. Explain that this is the answer you get when you subtract the handful he or she took from the bowl from the amount that was in the bowl to begin with. Explain that this process is called subtracting. To take something away is to subtract it from the original amount.

You can use dice in a similar fashion, as you can also

use plastic straws, plastic spoons, macaroni, and a variety of other household items.

If your child experiences difficulty in retaining basic addition facts, you might want to use the multiplication table in Appendix C for addition purposes. Please see the special note in Appendix C for this additional practice.

Next, let's take the addition and subtraction skills we have addressed thus far and make them pencil and paper activities. Children need to be able to take the skills they learn by using manipulatives and put them to use practically.

Take a look at this problem: Add 23 and 16. First you need to teach your child *how* to set this up. You need to show your child that the numbers to be added are to be placed one on top of the other like this:

$$\begin{array}{r} 23 \\ + 16 \\ \hline \end{array}$$

The next step is to show your child how to add the columns. Starting from the right side, first add the ones column, the 3 and the 6. When you arrive at the answer, which is 9, place the 9 at the bottom of that same column like this:

$$\begin{array}{r} 23 \\ + 16 \\ \hline 9 \end{array}$$

Next we add the numbers in the left column (known as the "tens column," the 2 and the 1. Then place the answer, 3, at the bottom of that column. The finished problem should look like this:

$$\begin{array}{r} 23 \\ + 16 \\ \hline 39 \end{array}$$

Here are several more example problems to try with your child before encouraging individual practice. Notice that there will be no carrying or regrouping at this point as the intent is to only help your child adjust to adding columns. One skill at a time is usually enough to challenge a child.

Try these with your child, providing as much assistance as necessary:

25	13	38
+ 44	+ 25	+ 61

Be sure to instruct your child to always go from right to left when adding. After you have finished the above examples with your child, ask your child to try these next problems alone:

1. 71 + 16
2. 32 + 45
3. 66 + 12
4. 50 + 37
5. 13 + 75
6. 22 + 41
7. 81 + 16
8. 39 + 20
9. 55 + 24
10. 63 + 14

Now that addition has been addressed, your child is probably ready to understand that we can subtract vertically as well. Here are several examples to explore with your child. Remember to explain to your child that the same rules apply to subtraction as addition. The only difference is that we will now be subtracting the numbers instead of adding them. Again, instruct your child to subtract from right to left.

Here are the examples:

$$75 - 44 \qquad 49 - 27 \qquad 24 - 12$$

Once you have completed the examples above, ask your child to try this next set of problems. Once again, feel free to assist when necessary:

1. 88 – 26
2. 73 – 21
3. 59 – 28
4. 46 – 13
5. 61 – 40
6. 95 – 35
7. 33 – 11
8. 78 – 56
9. 84 – 31
10. 52 – 41

Your only obstacle is your imagination. Most importantly, you need to continue explaining terms and concepts and using important key words throughout the learning process to reinforce skills. The more you use the terminology of the concepts you are working on, the more likely your child is to remember and use those same terms. Repetition is the key to success. Just be careful to provide a variety of activities to avoid losing your child's interest as you progress.

Here are a series of five challenge problems using addition and subtraction for you and your child to ponder. These problems are difficult in nature and not mandatory for the completion of this chapter. You might want to try them with your child if you are so inclined, however do not feel that you must complete them to move on.

1. $347 + 49 + 6022 = ?$
2. $3245 + 378 + 99 = ?$
3. $5655 + 3418 + 29 = ?$
4. $725 - 377 = ?$
5. $1019 - 463 = ?$

For additional practice and critical thinking in this area, please see chapter 10.

Now that you and your child have finished the basic operations of adding and subtracting whole numbers, your next step is multiplication. Although multiplying is merely an extended version of addition, the concept is sometimes a little more difficult for a child to comprehend. Just keep in mind that the manipulatives can help your child "see" what is actually happening once you begin.

CHAPTER
three

Learning to Multiply

Learning to multiply requires a child's complete comprehension of basic addition and subtraction skills. Since multiplication is merely an extension of addition, mastery of addition and subtraction skills first is extremely critical. In the presentation of multiplication, you'll probably find the operational counting sticks in Appendix B helpful to teach basic multiplication concretely. Children seem to learn more quickly and easily when they can *see* what they are learning. Most children are visual learners and will learn more readily through manipulative approaches, so the counting sticks are extremely beneficial.

Using Appendix B and your operational counting sticks, discuss the meaning of "multiplication" with your child before you actually begin teaching the concept. The basic definition of multiplication is to increase or get larger or grow in number. Use this as a basis for discussion with your child.

Once you have completed this task, line up the counting sticks by size on your table, from smallest to largest, left to right. Keep the groups separated so you can easily access any number that you might need. The different colors make it easier for both you and your child to identify and keep separate the ten differently numbered counting sticks necessary for this exercise.

Here's an easy example to help you understand how the operational counting sticks are used in multiplication problems. Let's say we want to multiply 2 times 3. Take two of the pink (3) counting sticks and lay them end to end. Next, try to find the counting stick that measures the same length as the two pink sticks. The only counting stick that is the same length is the orange (6) counting stick. Notice that the orange counting stick is the equivalent of the number six. Therefore, 6 is your answer.

You will probably want to demonstrate this problem for your child to help explain the concept of multiplication. After you have done this, try the following problem with your child. Ask your child to multiply 2 times 2. Understand that what you are asking him or her to find is two twos. Have your child first lay two of the blue (2) counting sticks end to end first. Next ask your child to find the counting stick that is the same length as the two he or she just put together. Your child should, after a reasonable period of time, be able to come up with the yellow (4) counting stick. Your child should lay the yellow stick right next to the two blue sticks to verify that they are indeed the same length. Remember to be patient during this exercise, as it usually takes awhile for most children to fully grasp this concept.

Here are some other problems you might like to have your child try using the operational counting sticks:

1. 3 × 2 or **three twos**
2. 2 × 4 or **two fours**
3. 3 × 4 or **three fours**
4. 3 × 1 or **three ones**
5. 1 × 4 or **one four**
6. 5 × 2 or **five twos**
7. 5 × 1 or **five ones**
8. 2 × 3 or **two threes**
9. 4 × 2 or **four twos**
10. 1 × 1 or **one one**

Don't feel you need to limit yourself to the operational counting sticks. You can use buttons, coins, or even tooth-picks in these exercises; just be sure to emphasize that you are using *groups* to multiply, since groups are the funda-mental element in multiplication.

Once you have addressed the basic concept of multi-plication, you should then approach a problem-solving atmosphere with your child. It is most important to relate real-life situations to each skill so that your child begins to realize that there is, in fact, a purpose to each and every skill he or she is learning.

Let's take a look at a very basic example of multipli-cation in a real-life situation: Steven likes to save pennies. He has 3 jars that are filled to the top. Each jar holds 50 pennies. How many pennies does he have altogether? To answer this problem, you would simply multiply 50 by 3. The answer, 150, would then tell you how many pennies Steven has altogether. I do not recommend this problem for your child, however, because it involves using a two-digit number. I just wanted to demonstrate the approach we will be using to attack problem solving with multiplication.

Now, let's try a problem together. Hopefully, your child will begin to see that it is very similar to addition. If not, you might want to point out that it is similar in concept. Present the situation to your child like this: "You have three cups. There are two jellybeans in each cup. How many jellybeans do you have altogether?" You might even want to demonstrate this problem concretely by physically using the jellybeans. Use three cups and place two jellybeans in each cup. Allow your child to count them to see that there are six altogether. Now use the operational counting sticks to demonstrate the same concept. You might also want to once again use an electronic calculator to prove your answer. However, you must emphasize that a calculator is only to be used to check your answers.

Ask your child to select three of the blue (2) counting sticks and lay them end to end. Next, ask your child to find the counting stick that is just as long as the three blue sticks are together. Your child should select the orange (6) counting stick. The answer verifies the problem and substantiates the jellybean approach to the problem.

Now let's try another situation. Present the following problem to your child: "Mommy has two jars on the counter filled with flour and sugar. There are two cups in each jar. How many cups are in the jars altogether?"

Again, you will want to have your child select the appropriate counting sticks to solve the problem. Your child should select two blue (2) counting sticks and lay them end to end. Next he or she should find the counting stick that is the same length as the two blue (2) sticks are together. If your child is correct, he or she will select the yellow (4) counting stick. You will then want to discuss the answer with your child. Be sure to discuss the fact that two multiplied by two is four. Be sure to include in your discussion the fact that you can add two and two and arrive at the same result. It is important for your child to see the relationship between addition and multiplication.

Here's another situation to present and discuss with your child: "Daddy has four containers of motor oil in the garage. Each container has one quart of oil in it. How many quarts are there altogether?"

Again, have your child to select the appropriate counting sticks to solve the problem. Your child should select four of the brown (1) counting sticks and lay them end to end. Next he or she should find the counting stick that is the same length as the four brown (1) sticks are together. He or she should find that the yellow (4) counting stick is the same length. You will then want to discuss the fact that four times one is four and the yellow (4) counting stick is equal to the number four.

Here's one last problem to try before attempting the concept of multiplication without the benefit of a real-life situation. "There are four rose bushes in front of the house. Each rose bush has two roses on it. How many flowers are on the rose bushes altogether?"

Ask your child to select the appropriate counting sticks to solve the problem. Your child should select four blue (2) counting sticks for this problem. Next, your child should lay the sticks end to end. He or she should then try to find the counting stick that measures the same length. He or she should find the black (8) counting stick for his answer. Discuss the answer with your child, as well as the entire multiplication problem. It's important for your child to understand that the situation he or she has just solved is the same as multiplying four by two.

Next, present several multiplication problems without the benefit of real-life situations. Ask your child to attempt the following multiplication problems and feel free to assist as much as you feel necessary. At this point, providing a lot of assistance will not interfere with the learning process. Children learn at different rates and some will require more assistance initially to acquire new skills. Work with your child on the following:

1. 3×2
2. 2×5
3. 7×1
4. 3×3
5. 4×2
6. 2×2
7. 1×5
8. 4×1
9. 1×1
10. 5×2

Now that we have mastered the skill of single-digit multiplication, let's try multiplying a two-digit number by a one-digit number.

Before we begin multiplying, complete the multiplication table in Appendix C. It's a great idea to use the operational counting sticks to complete the activity, since this method helps your child become increasingly comfortable with the skill of basic multiplication. Once you have completed this activity, you should then proceed with the balance of this chapter.

Allow your child to use this table until such time that he or she becomes comfortable with multiplication facts. It's okay to allow your child to use this table as much as necessary. Your child will eventually wean him- or herself from it as time goes by, but you should not expect your child to memorize it. Multiplication flash cards will also help your child learn the table more rapidly and, should you decide to go this route, be sure to practice the flash-cards daily. Daily reinforcement leads to mastery of the skill. Remember, if your child begins to tire of any particular activity, stop immediately. You can always return to it another day!

Have your child keep the multiplication table nearby while he or she is working on the next series of problems. The first is a simple problem that involves no carrying of digits.

Take a look at this problem:

$$\begin{array}{r} 23 \\ \times\ 3 \\ \hline \end{array}$$

Have your child write this problem on a piece of paper. The objective is to teach your child to multiply from right to left just as we did with addtion and subtraction. First, have your child multiply the three in 23 by the multiplier 3. You should allow your child to use either the operational counting sticks or the multiplication table from Appendix C for this process.

When your child arrives at the correct answer, 9, show him or her, on the paper, where the response should be placed:

$$\begin{array}{r} 23 \\ \times\ 3 \\ \hline 9 \end{array}$$

Explain that the reason you are placing the 9 under the three is that you first multiplied by the three, directly above it.

Next you will want to have your child multiply the two in 23 by the multiplier 3. Again you should allow your child to use whichever method he or she prefers. You will then want to show your child that he should place his answer, 6, in front of the 9 in his answer:

$$\begin{array}{r} 23 \\ \times\ 3 \\ \hline 69 \end{array}$$

You will want to explain to your child that the reason he or she is placing the 6 in front of the 9 is that the number 2 that he or she just multiplied by is in front of the 3 he or she first multiplied by. The sequence of numbers in the answer must match the sequence of numbers in the problem he or she just multiplied. Therefore, the correct answer is 69. You might want to allow your child to check the answer using a calculator just to verify that it was done correctly.

Here's another problem to try using the same technique:

$$\begin{array}{r} 14 \\ \times\ 2 \\ \hline \end{array}$$

Once again, after your child has written the problem on his paper, you will want to explain to your child that he or she will first want to multiply the four in 14 by the multiplier 2. After showing your child where to place the response in the answer, have him or her then multiply the one in 14 by the multiplier 2. Again, show your child where the answer is to be placed and why. The correct answer is 28.

Once again, you should allow your child to check the answer using a simple calculator. I do not endorse allowing your child to use a calculator to solve the problems, however, as a system of checking it is rather painless and rather effective.

The reason I do not endorse using the calculator to solve is actually twofold. First of all, there is no challenge in solving problems when you can electronically compute solutions. Second, and most important, you deny your child learning the most basic of skills when you allow your child to use a calculator. I always tell my students that the electronic calculator is an inferior version of the calculator they have built in between their ears and, like most computers, will function best when they've had a lot of practice using it.

Here are a series of problems you can try with your child before moving on to the next section (multiplying a two-digit number by a one-digit number with carrying):

1. 22 × 4
2. 13 × 3
3. 34 × 2
4. 47 × 1
5. 11 × 5
6. 24 × 2
7. 41 × 3
8. 59 × 1
9. 31 × 4
10. 31 × 5

Next, let's go one step further and multiply a two-digit number by a one-digit number that involves carrying (or regrouping as it is sometimes called). In essence, we will really be doing the same thing we were just doing with one exception. We will now have answers that involve larger numbers that do not fit into our answer.

Let's take a look at this problem so you can see exactly what this involves:

$$
\begin{array}{r}
37 \\
\times\ 5 \\
\hline
\end{array}
$$

When your child multiplies the 7 in 37 by the multiplier 5, he or she will not know what to do with both the 3 and the 5 in 35. Explain to your child that there is only room for the one's digit of the number in the answer. Your child will need to "carry" the ten's digit over to the next column and add it in when he or she has completed the multiplication in that column.

In other words, have your child first multiply the 7 in 37 by the multiplier 5. Once this is completed, ask your child to write the answer on paper. You should then instruct your child to place the one's digit of that number in his or her answer under the 5.

Next you will want to have your child place the ten's digit, the 3 above the 3 in 37. Tell your child you are placing it there so you don't forget about it. You will need to use it later, but for the time being, you want to be able to keep track of where you are placing the numbers.

Now, you will want to have your child multiply the 3 in 37 by the multiplier 5. When your child arrives at the correct answer, ask him or her to write this answer down.

Now you will want to remind your child of the 3 that he or she carried from the last problem. Remind your child that you were placing it on top of the other 3 so he or she would remember to use it later. Later has now come and he or she will need to use the number to finish the problem.

Explain to your child that the answer 15 arrived at by multiplying the 3 in 37 by the multiplier 5 is incomplete. Your child will now need to add the 3 he carried to the 15 to finish off the problem.

Show your child exactly where he or she will need to

place this number in his answer. Therefore, the correct answer should be 185. You might even want to let your child again use a calculator to check the answer.

The chances are good that your child will still be a bit confused by this procedure, but you know how the saying goes, "Practice makes perfect." The more you practice this technique with your child, the better your child should become at mastering this skill.

Let's try another problem of the same kind. Remember the carrying process is not an easy one to comprehend, so be patient with this skill.

Take a look at the problem below:

$$\begin{array}{r} 45 \\ \times\ 6 \\ \hline \end{array}$$

First you are going to want to instruct your child to multiply the 5 in 45 by the multiplier 6. Using the multiplication table, your child should find that the answer to the first part of this problem should be 30. You will want to instruct your child to remember since there are two digits in the number, he or she will need to use the one's digit in the answer and carry over the ten's digit to the next column. In other words, the 0 goes in the answer and the 3 gets carried to the ten's column.

Next your child will need to multiply the 4 in 45 by the multiplier 6. Again, using the multiplication table, your child should be able to locate the answer 24. However, this should not be written into your child's answer yet. Remind your child that he or she has to add in to this answer the amount that was carried over, in this case the 3. Once your child has added the 3 to the 24, the final result of 27 then should be written into the answer.

Your child's final answer should be 270. Time and

care should be given to the carrying over process. Unlike multiplying a single-digit number by another single-digit number, this process involves a great deal more. It may take some time for your child to master this skill, so again your patience is a key player here. You will want to spread out, over a period of days, the presentation and practice of this skill. Remember that practicing over a period of time provides more reinforcement for your child at mastering any and all mathematics skills.

Here are several more problems of the same variety to provide practice for your child using "carrying" in multiplication. Once again, this skill is often called "regrouping":

1. 38 × 4
2. 16 × 6
3. 24 × 5
4. 43 × 7
5. 27 × 3
6. 19 × 2
7. 33 × 5
8. 46 × 4
9. 52 × 8
10. 25 × 6

By this point, your child should be well into getting the grasp of multiplication. You should feel free at this point to expand the type of problems you are doing with your child. From this point on, there is nothing new for your child to learn in multiplication that has not already been covered. Multiplication from this point on really does not get more involved. True, the problems get longer, but the only advanced skill necessary for successfully completing multiplication involves carrying. Perhaps you will want to address other basic skills with your child before you venture further in multiplication.

You are attempting to provide your child with a well-rounded mathematics background, the foundation of which involves basic skills. It is definitely in the best interest of your child to keep it simple. I would definitely recommend waiting to explore multiplication further until you have first successfully explored the other basic skills with your child.

But for those of you who feel your child is up to a challenge, try these:

1. 38×57
2. 44×75
3. 52×83
4. 19×40
5. 55×79

For additional practice and critical thinking in this area, see chapter 10.

Now that we have finished an introduction to multiplication, we are going to move on to basic division. You should mention to your child that division is the opposite of multiplication. Multiplication is an operation that involves expanding, whereas division is an operation that involves decreasing or breaking down into smaller groups. "Taking away" is also a key phrase to assist your child in the understanding of division. Division needs to be kept in perspective relative to multiplication and subtraction, and the more you incorporate these "names" into your discussions with your child, the more likely he or she is to see the connections.

Learning to Divide

In exploring the concept of division, explain to your child that it is the process of taking away numbers in equal groups. Division is the process by which we find equal groups that can be deducted from another number. As multiplication is to addition so is division to subtraction. Basically, division is a quicker process for subtracting larger numbers.

Explain to your child that what you will be trying to do is to find how many times one number goes evenly into another number and how much you will have left over, if anything. Here's a simple example:

"Mommy has eight tulip bulbs. Each planter will hold two bulbs. How many planters will Mommy be able to fill?" The problem is asking you to do the following: $8 \div 2 = ?$ First try solving this problem using the operational counting sticks. Use the black (8) counting stick and the blue (2) counting stick. Ask your child how many blue sticks laid end to end will be the same length as the black stick.

Your child will find that exactly four of the blue sticks will be the same length as the black stick.

Here's another situation to try. "Daddy has ten shoes in his closet. Each shoe box holds two shoes. How many pairs of shoes does Daddy have in the closet?"

Once again, direct your child to select the following counting sticks to help solve this problem. Have your child select the red (10) and the blue (2) counting sticks. Ask your child how many blue counting sticks it will take to be just as long as the red counting stick? You should feel free to assist your child as necessary. Your child should find that it will take exactly five blue counting sticks to measure the same length as the red counting stick. Explain to your child in simple language "You have just divided two into ten. It went exactly five times, therefore there are five pairs of shoes in Daddy's closet."

Here's another problem to attempt with your child: "Mommy has six cookies she wants to split evenly with her daughter (or son). How many cookies will each person get?" In other words, we are looking to divide six by two. You will need the counting sticks to once again help you solve the problem. First, your child should find the orange (6) counting stick. Next, he or she should find how many blue (2) counting sticks laid end to end will be the same as the orange counting stick. When your child has done this, he or she should find that the correct answer is three, since it took three blue counting sticks to measure the same length as the orange counting stick. At this point, you might want to show your child how division is done on a calculator. Again, reinforce with your child that you are using the calculator only as a means of checking, or verifying, your answer.

Now, I would recommend that you try the following

division problems with your child using the counting sticks and the calculator as a means of checking answers. If you feel the need to make the problems into more tangible real-life situations, do not be afraid to do so. Using real-life situations does *not* diminish the learning of the basic skill.

1. $6 \div 2$
2. $3 \div 1$
3. $4 \div 4$
4. $10 \div 5$
5. $8 \div 2$
6. $5 \div 1$
7. $9 \div 3$
8. $8 \div 4$
9. $10 \div 2$
10. $6 \div 3$

Now what happens when one number does not divide evenly into another? This is the tough part of division for children. Look at the problem below and see what happens:

$$10 \div 3 = ?$$

Using the counting sticks, your child will find that three pink (3) counting sticks are not enough, yet four pink counting sticks are too many. Show your child that three pink counting sticks are the correct answer because four is too many. However, he or she is not finished with the problem since three does not go evenly into ten. You will then want to direct your child to find the counting stick that will finish the problem. He or she should find that the brown (1) counting stick completes the problem. Explain to your child that brown, or one, is the remainder or the leftover in the problem. The correct way to write the answer to the problem is: $10 \div 3 = 3$ R1. The R represents the remainder.

Now have your child try these to see how well he or she understands the concept:

1. $10 \div 4$
2. $9 \div 2$
3. $8 \div 3$
4. $5 \div 2$
5. $7 \div 3$
6. $9 \div 4$
7. $8 \div 5$
8. $7 \div 2$
9. $10 \div 6$
10. $8 \div 6$

For additional practice and critical thinking in this area, see chapter 10. This might also be a good time to consult Appendix E, which provides your child with the opportunity to try his or her hand at some challenging problems in addition, subtraction, multiplication, and division.

Now that the four basic operations have been covered, we are going to move into everyday experiences that involve numbers and a child's basic mathematical ability to understand and utilize those numbers. The most important of all these skills is money. Because we deal with this skill daily, it needs to be addressed in order to help your child understand how math and money are closely related.

CHAPTER
five

Money, Money, Money

Money seems to be a topic many children initially have difficulty understanding. It stands to reason when you think about the value of American coins and the lack of any relationship based on their size. Is it logical that a dime should be smaller than a penny when in reality it is worth ten times as much? Or what about a nickel? Shouldn't it be one-half the size of the dime and not vice versa? When you actually stop to think about it, as far as the American money system goes, it really doesn't make a lot of "cents" and it should be easy to understand why it can be so confusing to youngsters.

Before we even begin working with coins, I recommend using Appendix D. The coins in Appendix D should be cut out and colored as indicated so your child can have a fun activity before plunging into the mathematical aspects of money. Remember to allow ample time for this activity. You might also want to discuss the value of the coins with your child while you are cutting out and coloring them to provide a foundation for this section on money.

You will also want to consult Appendix B in that we will be using the counting sticks to help your child understand the concept of coin value. Make ten brown (1) counting sticks (which will represent the penny), two silver (5) counting sticks (which will represent the nickel) and one red (10) counting stick (which will represent the dime) for this exercise. This should help your child interrelate the coins and their values regardless of their sizes.

Before you even begin working with the coins, be sure to clarify to your child that five brown counting sticks (penny) are equal to one silver counting stick (nickel). Ten brown counting sticks (penny) are equal to one red counting stick (dime). Two silver counting sticks (nickel) are equal to one red counting stick (dime). However, it will be difficult to convince your child that five brown counting sticks (penny) and one silver counting stick (nickel) also equal one red counting stick (dime).

While you are working with the coin activities, use the counting sticks first, the cut out paper coins second, and finally real coins for each of the following situations. You might even want to make a counting stick that is equal in length to twenty-five brown counting sticks (penny) so that you have the equivalent of one quarter. Remember, however, that the concept of the quarter will probably be most difficult for your child to understand.

It is very important for your child to understand that there are five pennies in one nickel and two nickels in one dime. This in itself will probably take more time than any other math skill your child will encounter. Remember to be patient and to break down the activities into small doses. Daily reinforcement is far more significant than overkill in any one given day.

The best approach to teaching money and the values

of the coins is to work with the coins individually before trying to tie them together. What better place to begin than with the penny? Before you begin, you will need to have ten pennies to manipulate. You will also want to have ten brown counting sticks. Please notice that the counting sticks are colored to somewhat represent the penny and the nickel to help make the transition to real money somewhat easier. The concrete presentations make the most sense to children since they are easiest to understand. Trying to explain a skill to a child without the benefit of a manipulative is very much like trying to get someone to switch long distance carriers without showing the person what he or she will save. You need to show children what you are talking about!

Beginning with the penny, make sure you have at least ten pennies on hand to manipulate. For this exercise, you will also want to have a nickel, two dimes, and a quarter handy as well. First, lay out the counting sticks on the table and tell your child that "we are going to pretend that this is money." The brown counting stick represents 1 cent, the silver counting stick represents 5 cents, and the red counting stick represents 10 cents. Then, lay out coins on your kitchen table with the five pennies grouped together, then the nickel, then the two dimes, and finally the quarter. Explain the value of each coin based on "cents." For example, a nickel is 5 cents and a dime is 10 cents. Children need to understand that all coins will eventually break down to pennies.

Next, use the following example to show how the coins can be used together. First, ask your child which counting sticks could add up to seventeen. Then ask your child which coins they might use to show 17 cents. Help them by showing a dime, a nickel, and two pennies and actually count the "cent" value of each coin to reach the total of 17 cents.

Now try the same process for each of the following coin values until you feel your child understands how the coins work together. Try 8 cents, 14 cents, 23 cents, 27 cents, 30 cents, and finally 37 cents. Use your imagination if you need to continue this exercise to help your child comprehend the value of coins.

Should you feel your child would benefit from more practice you might want to try this: Remove all counting sticks and coins from the table. In front of your child, place a red (10) counting stick, a silver (5) counting stick, and three brown (1) counting sticks. Ask your child how much there is altogether. You may assist in arriving at the answer. When you have finished this try the same exercise with coins. Place a dime, a nickel, and three pennies on the table. Then ask your child how much money there is altogether. Feel free to assist by counting the values of the coins out loud with your child. When you reach the total (18 cents in this case), repeat the answer several times to reinforce the solution.

You might want to try this several times just for practice with your child. Understand that the more practice and the more reinforcement you provide, the more your child is apt to remember. There's an old saying that goes, "If you throw enough mud against the wall, some of it will stick!" The same applies here.

After you have utilized these exercises, you might want to space your "workouts" with money. I advise working with your child on these skills daily, but always in small doses. Review the skills you have taught spread out over days and then weeks and you will find that your child will retain much, much more. Once you feel your child has mastered understanding the values of coins there are many ways you can reinforce your child's knowledge of coins and their values.

Find the food section in your local newspaper. The reason I suggest this particular section is that it is the section most loaded with coin-value examples that easily lend themselves to additional practice with coins. Make sure you have plenty of coins on hand for these exercises. Now, ask your child to find an item he or she would like to buy and then ask your child to select the coins necessary to purchase the item. You might even want to have your child select several items and select the coins necessary to make the purchase. Finally, incorporate a trip to the supermarket to make the actual purchase. Never underestimate the value of real-life experiences and the impact they have on reinforcing skills.

You could actually set up a replica of a store either in your kitchen or family room and set up grocery-type items with price tags on them. Give your child a certain amount of money to spend and send him or her on a shopping spree. The only limitation to this exercise is your imagination.

Another exercise you might want to try is to take your child to a local discount store and allow him or her to select one or two items for purchase. Next, go to the register and allow your child to make the purchase with the coins he or she selects. (You will have to supplement the tax portion of the purchase and perhaps you might even want to explain what sales tax is at a very basic level.) Most cashiers and stores encourage this type of activity. It's an easy way to make the exercise meaningful and fun at the same time!

Another activity involves the use of vending machines. Once again, the use of coins is significant in terms of making a purchase and the importance of real-life experiences. Encourage your child to make these purchases instead of making the purchases for him or her so that your child can get used to dealing with coins and reinforcing their values and interrelationships.

Once you have reached the point where you feel your child has mastered coins to this level, you might also want to introduce the half-dollar. Although it is not a commonly used coin, it would still be a good idea to acquaint your child with it. Silver dollars and Susan B. Anthony dollars are also rare, yet worth discussing. However, I would wait until you have finished practice with "paper" money before discussing dollar coins with your child.

Paper money should really not be addressed until such time as your child is completely comfortable manipulating coins. It is also a good idea not to mix paper and coins until your child is comfortable with each separately. Combinations can come later.

Exercises with paper money should be limited to ones, fives, tens, and twenties. Utilize similar examples to the coin problems to help familiarize your child with paper money. It will be substantially easier in that the bills are marked with their numeric value. Also the sizes are uniform so children will be less apt to confuse the value based on the size of the bill. The numeric value of the bill will be enough to help your child identify the bill and its value.

A simple game of Monopoly® can help reinforce dollar values for your child. Other money-type board games are also great tools for learning. LIFE® is another board game that lends itself well to this concept.

The next logical step to learning money involves combining paper money with coins. Laying out bills on your kitchen table with coins allows your child the opportunity to learn such values as $1.33 or $7.47. You might even want to ask your child to get $6.75 from the paper and coins lying on the table. Once again, the more practice you give your child, the more proficient he or she will become.

A trip to the local discount store is appropriate for purchasing an item between one and five dollars. Allow your child to go to the register to pay for the item. After the cashier rings up the item (including tax), allow your child to count out the money to the cashier. This will provide your child not only the opportunity of demonstrating money skills but also the proper way to behave in such a setting.

Understanding money is significant in that it spills over into so many other areas of math. Operations with money are similar to basic operations with whole numbers, except that you are dealing with decimal values. The basic operations work predominantly the same way, except there are basic rules dealing with decimals that come up later in this book. Just remember that decimals and money are synonymous.

The next topic we address is time. As difficult as that may seem today since so many of the clocks manufactured are digital, the basic knowledge of time, how it works, what it means, and how society uses it cannot be underestimated. But to actually use it, your child will first need to understand it.

CHAPTER
six

A Matter of Time

The concept of time is often difficult to teach and sometimes equally as difficult for children to grasp, primarily because time does not use base ten numbers. Rather, time is based upon factors of sixty since there are sixty seconds in one minute and sixty minutes in one hour. What makes the concept of time even more difficult is that you have to begin counting from twelve. These factors are important to realize when teaching time, so patience is once again of utmost importance.

Since so many of today's clocks are digital, you and your child will need a clock with a face, hands, and numbers to learn this concept. If you do not have a clock available, you can use the clock face in Appendix F. You might even want to have your child color it and cut it out as a beginning activity. I would even recommend coloring the minute hand and the hour hand different colors to make it easier to distinguish between the two.

First explain to your child the features of the clock. Your child needs to understand that there are five minutes between each number on the face of the clock. Your child also needs to understand that the numbers on the face of the clock are only actually read as the hours and not the minutes. You should explain that to determine the number of minutes past the current hour you multiply the number on the face of the clock by five.

To begin teaching the function and operation of the clock, you need to have a clock in front of you and your child to use as an example of what you will be explaining. First, show your child that each number on the face of the clock represents the hour. Tell your child that when the hour hand is pointing to that number then it is that hour of the day.

Take turns turning the hour hand to different positions on the face of the clock and asking your child what hour it is when the hour hand is in each position. Be sure you have asked each hour at least once before moving on to the minute hand.

We face an entirely different set of standards when we begin to address the minute hand. Explain to your child that each number on the face of the clock, when referring to minutes, is a multiple of five minutes. For example, when the minute hand is on the two, this represents two fives, or ten minutes. When the minute hand is on the six, this represents six fives, or thirty minutes. If your child hasn't already mastered the skill, this might be a good place to teach your child how to count by fives. Feel free to demonstrate the skill of counting by fives until you feel your child is catching on. Then count by fives with him or her and finally let your child count by fives alone until he or she is comfortable with this process. If necessary, have your child count by fives up to sixty at least half a dozen times to be sure he or she is relatively comfortable with the procedure.

Next, you will want to deal with the minute hand in depth. In order not to confuse your child, first deal with five-minute increments only on the face of the clock. Do not ask your child how many minutes unless you place the minute hand directly on a number. The concept is difficult enough to explain without complicating it more than necessary.

Spend time with your child discussing how many minutes past the hour are involved when the minute hand is directly on a number. It would probably be a good idea to do several examples for your child so he or she gets an idea of exactly what you are trying to convey. You will need to spend a fair amount of time on this particular skill because your child is likely to have a little more difficulty with this than he or she did with the hour hand.

Ask your child how many minutes past the hour it would be if the minute hand was on the two. Then on the five. On the nine. On the four. Be sure you cover all digits at least two or three times before putting this skill to rest. You might even want to consider spreading this practice over the course of several days to make it a little more fun. And, of course, there is absolutely nothing wrong with working on this unit while you are simultaneously working on another unit. I would not recommend, however, working on this unit while you are also working on the unit of money. Since both units are rather difficult from a child's point of view, you want to spare frustrating your child.

Once you have surpassed the concept of helping your child understand the minutes on the face of the clock, you should address the minutes on the clock when the minute hand is *not* directly on a number. You should explain that there are exactly five minutes between each number on the face of a clock.

Next, tell your child that it is necessary to determine how many minutes there are up to the number just before the minute hand. Then your child can count and add on the number of minutes past the number on the face of the clock.

It's important to spend an ample amount of time discussing the number of minutes on the face of the clock when the minute hand is in various positions. You can have your child first count by fives and then add on the additional minutes past the number on the face of the clock. Once again, you might consider spreading this out over the course of several days to prevent unnecessary frustration.

Once your child has an accurate understanding of how the minute hand works, try combining the minute hand with the hour hand to complete the task of telling time by the hour and minute. Once again, start slowly, presenting several examples and explaining each example as you go.

Consider the following example: "When the hour hand is on the four and the minute hand is on the two, what time is it?" First explain to your child that since the hour hand is on the four, it is four o'clock. And since the minute hand is on the two, it is two fives, or ten minutes, past the hour. Therefore the time is ten minutes after four o'clock.

One more example: "The hour hand is on the six and the minute hand is on the nine. What time is it?" Since the hour hand is on the six it must be six o'clock. Since the minute hand is on the nine, it is nine fives, or forty-five minutes, past the hour. Therefore it is forty-five minutes past six o'clock.

Now try several examples with your child to see how well he or she is grasping the concept. The chances are pretty good that this skill is going to require time to perfect. Once again, it is probably a good idea to spread this out over several days, doing a few exercises each day, until your child gets the idea. It would probably be a good idea to work on this daily for just a brief period of time over several weeks. It is important to understand that the more complex the skill, the more reinforcement the skill is apt to require and the more time it will take. Just remember to be patient!

When addressing the issue of time, a discussion of adding and subtracting periods of time is also necessary. In other words, we are also going to look at elapsed time. For example, "If you start working on a chore at 9:15 A.M. and finish the task by 11:30 A.M., how much time was spent on the task?" The significance here is actually rather important. This skill assists a person's understanding of train, bus and airplane schedules, as well as a number of other everyday activities that involve understanding the concept of how much time has passed.

Let's take a look at elapsed time and how to teach your child this concept. You may want to explain to your child that we will be looking at "time that has gone by" or "how much time has passed"—two key phrases that are sure to assist your child in understanding elapsed time. We can start with a very basic example. Let's say you leave the house in the morning to drive the kids to school. You leave at 8:00 A.M. exactly and arrive at the school at exactly 8:15 A.M. How long did the trip take? Well, you and I know, but what about your child? Where would he or she begin to solve this?

The easiest way to address this problem is as follows: Tell your child to look at a clock to solve this problem. "If you left at 8:00 A.M. and arrived at 8:15 A.M., how many minutes did it take?" Tell your child to count, on the face of a clock, the number of minutes from 8:00 to 8:15. You will also want to explain to your child that A.M. represents morning and P.M. represents afternoon and evening. Since the entire problem is in the morning, the solution is found by simply subtracting the number of minutes in the original problem.

This may seem a little confusing to your child so let's try another example that looks at the same kind of situation. Pose this question to your child: "Jeff started cleaning his bedroom at 9:15 A.M. and finished the job at 9:45 A.M. How long did it take Jeff to clean his bedroom?"

Once again, we will need to subtract since we are talking about elapsed time or "time gone by." You can have your child, once again, look at the face of a clock and count the minutes (by increments of five) from 9:15 to 9:45. Or you can have your child subtract fifteen from forty-five. The answers should come out exactly the same. You can devise several more problems of this type if you feel your child needs to spend more time on this type of a problem.

The next type of time problem we are going to address involves overlapping. This is going to be a little more difficult for your child to understand, so no doubt it will also take more time and patience to master. In other words, moving from one hour into another hour time frame. Take a look at this problem: "Mom and Dad decided to drive to Grandma's house on Saturday. We left the house at 8:00 A.M. and arrived at Grandma's at 9:30 A.M. How long did the trip take?" How can you help your child begin to solve this problem?

Again, start with the face of a clock. First, your child needs to understand that every time the minute hand passes the twelve, another hour has passed. It is tremendously helpful to your child to break the problem down into parts, or sections, to make it easier to solve. So, starting at 8:00, one hour will pass when you reach 9:00. Next, address the remaining time by using the last example we discussed and subtracting the times (or count out the time by increments of five on the face of a clock). The period of time elapsed from 9:00 to 9:30 is exactly thirty minutes. Then you will need to tell your child that the time elapsed from 8:00 to 9:00 is one hour and the time elapsed from 9:00 to 9:30 is thirty minutes, or one-half hour so the *total* time elapsed is one hour and thirty minutes or one and one-half hours.

Let's try another example you can present to your child: "John and Mark are going on vacation together. They are flying from Los Angeles to Portland. Their plane leaves at 9:15 A.M. and arrives at 11:00 A.M. How long is their flight?"

Once again it will help to break down the problem into parts. I strongly encourage you to break down the problem by hour since this is a period of time that is a small enough increment for your child to work with. First, look at the first part of the problem. How much time has elapsed from 9:15 to 10:00? You can either have your child count by increments of five minutes to establish the answer of forty-five minutes or you can subtract. In order to subtract, you should show your child that since one hour equals sixty minutes, he or she can subtract using sixty in place of the one hour. In essence, your child will be subtracting fifteen minutes from sixty minutes to arrive at an answer of forty-five minutes. Now we will need to look at the remainder of the problem.

Now that we have established the period of forty-five minutes from 9:15 to 10:00, we need to address the remaining period of time, from 10:00 to 11:00. You can explain to your child that since the minute hand goes around the clock exactly one time, exactly one hour has gone by.

Now we take the forty-five minutes and the one hour and add them together to get our total flying time. The final answer is, therefore, one hour and forty-five minutes.

Here's another example you might want to try with your child: "Barbara and Tom have decided to drive to San Diego this weekend. They leave Los Angeles at 8:15 A.M. and arrive in San Diego at 10:45 A.M. How long did the drive to San Diego take?"

The first step in solving this problem is to split it up into parts. Using the face of a clock, we will first need to find the elapsed time from 8:15 to 9:00, since we do not want to cross over hours. Counting by increments of five minutes, your child will find that there are exactly forty-five minutes from 8:15 to 9:00.

Now we need to address the elapsed time from 9:00 to 10:00. Since we are making one complete rotation on the face of the clock, this constitutes exactly one hour.

Finally, we need to figure the elapsed time from 10:00 to 10:45. Once again, counting increments of five minutes, your child will find that there are exactly forty-five minutes from 10:00 to 10:45.

Now we need to combine our times to find the total trip time: The first block of time is forty-five minutes. The second block of time is one hour, and the third block of time is forty-five minutes. When we combine these figures, we have one hour and ninety minutes. The ninety-minute figure is apt to confuse your child, so try explaining it this way: "There are exactly sixty minutes in one hour. If we take this away from the ninety minutes, we will then have thirty minutes left." This way, it becomes a simple subtraction problem.

Now, to put it all together, we have one hour plus one hour plus thirty minutes, or a total of two hours and thirty minutes. So, the trip from Los Angeles to San Diego, by car, took exactly two hours and thirty minutes.

Now, believe it or not, there is another way to solve

this problem. It comes from the idea that one full rotation on the clock represents exactly one hour.

Let's reconsider the scenario: They left Los Angeles for San Diego at 8:15 and arrived in San Diego at 10:45, correct? Using the face of a clock, from 8:15 to 9:15 is exactly one hour. From 9:15 to 10:15 is exactly one hour. From 10:15 to 10:45 is thirty minutes.

If we were to combine these totals, we would also arrive at the same total elapsed time of two hours and thirty minutes.

You might want to present both methods to your child to see which is easier for him or her to understand and then pursue that method.

Here are several more examples you can use to help your child understand the idea of elapsed time. Find the elapsed time for each of the following:

1. From 1:15 P.M. to 2:30 P.M.
2. From 3:00 P.M. to 5:45 P.M.
3. From 8:30 A.M. to 10:00 A.M.
4. From 9:15 A.M. to 12:00 noon
5. From 4:20 P.M. to 7:00 P.M.
6. From 6:10 A.M. to 8:40 A.M.
7. From 11:30 A.M. to 1:15 P.M.
8. From 7:05 P.M. to 10:00 P.M.
9. From 12:00 noon to 3:35 P.M.
10. From 8:45 P.M. to 11:15 P.M.

Another aspect of time involves converting one increment to another increment of time. For example, how many minutes are there in two hours?

First you will need to explain to your child the following incremental equivalents:

1 hour = 60 minutes
1 minute = 60 seconds

Now that we have established the conversion rates, let's try a few simple problems with your child and see how this works. It's okay for your child to have the conversion rates in front of him or her while working on these. This will help your child learn the conversion rates and eventually he or she will not need them at all. Your child will automatically remember them.

Ask your child the following questions. Do not be afraid to assist if necessary until your child gets the idea. You will find yourself helping less and less with each problem he or she tries:

1. 3 minutes = _____ seconds
2. 1 hour = _____ minutes
3. 120 seconds = _____ minutes
4. 60 minutes = _____ hours
5. 3 hour = _____ minutes
6. 180 seconds = _____ minutes
7. 2 hours = _____ minutes
8. 5 minutes = _____ seconds
9. 60 seconds = _____ minutes
10. 1 hour = _____ seconds

You might even want to incorporate a stop watch to help demonstrate the changes from minutes to seconds and seconds to minutes. A stop watch will add the movement of time to further help establish the elapsed time we have been speaking of throughout this chapter.

You can easily add additional problems in the area of time if you feel your child needs additional practice.

It might be wise to purchase an inexpensive watch for your child to use for these exercises, however, I encourage you to purchase one that is *not* digital. You will need one that has a face with markings to assist your child in solving the types of problems presented throughout this chapter. Hopefully, owning a watch of his or her own will also encourage your child to want to tell time on a regular basis, as ownership often serves as a wonderful motivating tool.

For additional practice and critical thinking in this area, see chapter 10.

The concept of time is not limited to clocks. Increments of time, be it hours, minutes, or seconds, also translate into days, weeks, months, and years. It is therefore timely to next move into reading and interpreting calendars so your child can see the relationships that hours on his or her watch have with months on the calendar.

CHAPTER seven

Month by Month

The ability to read and understand a calendar is a skill that is often overlooked. It is actually rather difficult for a child to find the number of days, weeks, or months that have passed. What makes it so difficult is the fact that all months do not have the same number of days.

The first topic you should address with your child is the names of the months and number of days in each month. This, in itself, is likely to take some time. I would probably leave out the concept of "leap year," in that it is only going to confuse your child. Later on, you might want to address the topic of leap day and the reason we have leap year once every four years. The reason for leap day has to do with the rotation of the earth on its axis, which causes us to pick up one extra day every four years.

Let's first begin with the names of the months and the number of days in each month. It would be most helpful to have a large calendar to use for reference in this unit. Appendix G has a generic monthly calendar designed to help explain the concept of days, weeks, and months. I would encourage you to make twelve enlarged copies of the generic calendar to equal one full year so your child can color in the different days and make this a hands-on, fun activity. This is a perfect opportunity to help your child identify family birthdays, anniversaries, and other important family-related dates. It also leaves room for discussion about the fact that seven days equal one week and approximately four weeks equal one month. This conversation should take place while your child is coloring in the generic calendar.

After you have made the monthly calendar(s) with your child, you should discuss the days in the week with him or her. Explain that there are exactly seven days in each week. Take the time to go through the seven days: Sunday, Monday, Tuesday, Wednesday, Thursday, Friday, and Saturday. You probably should explain that there are twenty-four hours in one day, since we have already passed the unit on time and this will give you the opportunity to connect the last unit to this one. Connecting the information will help your child begin to see how all the various concepts are related.

After you have taken the time to discuss the days in the week, be sure that your child understands that one week consists of exactly seven days. Explain to your child that not every month has the same number of days. This may be difficult for your child to understand, but in time he or she will adjust to the theory and eventually remember how many days each of the specific months has. This is one reason that making twelve copies of the generic monthly calendar is so important.

Once you have reached this point and have had a general discussion with your child regarding days, weeks, and months, proceed to the topic of elapsed time or time passed. Just as with the concept of clock time, elapsed time applies to days, weeks, and months, too.

We will be looking at how many days have passed and accomplish this task either by actually counting the days on the calendar or by simple subtraction.

Take a look at this example, and ask your child: "Spring vacation begins on Friday, April 7th. Spring vacation ends on Sunday, April 16th. How many days long is spring vacation?" On a calendar, you could simply count the days from April 7th to April 16th. Or you could subtract seven from sixteen. Either way, you should have the same result.

It is probably a good idea to have your child actually count the days on a calendar for the additional practice of being exposed to the calendar. The more exposure your child actually has to a calendar, the more comfortable he or she will become with it.

Here are some other problems you might want to try with your child. Feel free to assist your child as long as necessary until he or she becomes comfortable handling the problems alone. You should, however, demonstrate both methods of solving this type of problem, counting the days and subtracting, to allow your child the opportunity of selecting the method that works best for him or her.

Here are some problems to try. Ask your child how many days have elapsed or passed in the following examples:

1. **From the 3rd to the 12th of the month**
2. **From the 11th to the 14th of the month**
3. **From the 18th to the 30th of the month**
4. **From the 6th to the 13th of the month**
5. **From the 14th to the 25th of the month**
6. **From the 1st to the 10th of the month**

7. From the 8th to the 20th of the month
8. From the 4th to the 14th of the month
9. From the 16th to the 30th of the month
10. From the 22nd to the 31st of the month

Another concept to address has to do with the number of weeks in a month. The concept of one week, or seven days, is one that needs to be explained to your child. You might want to address this from the angle that school days each week are Monday through Friday. Or you might want to connect certain tasks to specific days of the week, such as grocery shopping on Saturdays, to help your child make the correlation. Armed with the information that a week officially begins on a Sunday and officially ends on a Saturday, your child is likely to feel more comfortable with the terms "work week" and "weekend."

Another activity, mathematically, that could stimulate more discussion has to do with the number of specific days in a month. For example, you might want to ask your child, "when you have finished coloring and decorating your monthly calendars, how many Mondays are there in March? How many Saturdays are there in July?" Hopefully, your child will begin to see that these statistics change from month to month and also from year to year.

Ask your child to answer the following questions about the monthly calendar he or she made for July:

1. How many Mondays are there in July?
2. On what day does the month of July begin?
3. On what day of the week is July 14th?
4. How many Thursdays are there in July?
5. On what day does the month of July end?
6. What day comes after Tuesday?

7. **On what day of the week is July 27th?**
8. **How many Saturdays are there in July?**
9. **Which date is the middle of the month?**
10. **What day comes after Saturday?**
11. **On what day of the week is July 5th?**
12. **How many days are there altogether in July?**
13. **What day comes after Thursday?**

Ask your child to take a look at the following monthly calendar. Notice that there are missing dates. Ask your child to fill in the missing dates. (You might want to reproduce and enlarge this page on another piece of paper to make it easier for your child to work with the monthly calendar.)

MARCH

Sunday	Monday	Tuesday	Wednesday	Thursday	Friday	Saturday
		1	2	3		
6		8	9		11	
13	14			17		19
	21		23		25	
	28		30			

Remember there are thirty-one days in March. The monthly calendar ends on Thursday.

After your child has completed filling in the missing dates, ask him or her to answer the following questions:

1. How many Wednesdays are there in March?
2. On what day of the week is March 13th?
3. On what day of the week does March begin?
4. What day and date comes after March 11th?
5. On what day of the week is the last day of March?
6. What day and date comes before March 22nd?
7. How many Sundays are there in March?
8. On what day of the week is March 24th?
9. On what day of the week will April begin?
10. Which day and date is three days after March 4th?

Now that we have covered the topic of calendars and calendar dates, you can see that the possibilities for exploring this concept are seemingly endless. You can create so many activities with calendars focusing on religious holidays, family holidays, family vacations, and even school holidays.

Most importantly, remember to have fun with your child and with the activities. For additional practice and critical thinking in this area, see chapter 10.

The next topic is decimals. Because money involves decimals, you may want to quickly review money before jumping into decimals and their operations. You can never spend too much time on money anyway since it will be such an integral part of your child's life.

CHAPTER eight

Introduction to Decimals

The concept of decimals is most easily presented from the standpoint of money. Since chapter 5 covered money, you might want to review that chapter before moving forward in this chapter. Initially, we discuss the meaning of the decimal point, but then move on to demonstrate the appropriate usage of the decimal point, by converting to other number forms and by operating with them.

To make this as easy as possible, let's begin with a simple exercise involving money and decimal points. Explain to your child that all money less than one dollar can be written with a decimal point in front and that the decimal point represents number forms that are less than one.

For example, 52 cents written in decimal form is 0.52. It is not absolutely necessary to place the zero in front of the decimal point, however, it is usually a good idea since the number in front of the zero represents whole dollars. In this case, there are no whole dollars, only cents.

Here's another example: "Write 27 cents as a decimal number." The correct answer is 0.27. At this point, you might want to discuss the fact that there will always be two decimal places (or numbers) after the decimal point whenever we are discussing money.

The first place after the decimal point (in terms of money) is called the dimes position, and the second place after the decimal point is called the penny position. So when we change 27 cents to a decimal number, 0.27, this means there are two dimes and seven pennies.

You should also explain to your child that all numbers in front of the decimal point represent whole dollars. For example, if we were to write $3.48 as a decimal, we would write 3.48. This means there are three dollars, four dimes, and eight pennies.

Here's another example: "Write $6.19 as a decimal number." The correct answer is 6.19 because there are six dollars, one dime, and nine pennies. By the way, another way of presenting this problem would be to say, "How do you write six dollars and nineteen cents as a decimal number?" It does get a little more difficult this way, but you will want your child to feel comfortable with *both* expressions.

Here's one more example to try with your child before we proceed: "How would you write nine dollars and thirty cents as a decimal number?" The correct answer is 9.30. You might also want to explain to your child that the zero in 30 is only a "place holder." This means that the zero holds a place because there is no other number in that space.

Now is the time to ask your child to try some similar problems. You should ask your child to write an answer for each problem. Feel free to assist at the beginning since these problems do take practice. Ask your child to write each of these as a decimal number (you might want to do the first one for your child to show him or her what kind of answer you are looking for):

1. **Eighty-nine cents**
2. **Forty-four cents**
3. **Ninety cents**
4. **Fifty cents**
5. **Twenty-six cents**
6. **One dollar and ten cents**
7. **Four dollars and thirty-nine cents**
8. **Eight dollars and fifteen cents**
9. **Eleven dollars and sixty cents**
10. **Twenty-one dollars and twenty-one cents**

For the last five problems in the above exercise, you will want to show your child where to properly place the dollar sign in the answer. Explain to your child that most answers to mathematical problems require a "label" in the answer, such as $ or ¢. The reason for this is to show that you understand the problem and its answer. The label helps identify the answer. This way we all know what the answer is supposed to represent.

Now that your child has a basic understanding of decimal points as they relate to money, let's discuss how to add different sums of money.

Let's look at the simple addition of decimals. You might find it helpful to use the coins from Appendix D to assist in your explanation. You could also use real coins for this exercise if they are available. The usage of the coins helps reinforce the skill before explaining the rule for adding decimal numbers.

With the coins in front of you, ask your child to put

together a group of coins that total thirty-five cents. He or she should select one quarter and one dime. Now, ask your child to put together another group of coins that total twenty cents. Your child could select various combinations to arrive at twenty cents, however, the most logical would be either two dimes, or one dime and two nickels. Either way, have your child place the two groups next to each other.

Now ask your child how he or she might be able to determine how much money these would total altogether? Your child could push the two groups together and make one group of the coins and just count them, or he or she could count one group and continue counting with the second group. If he or she isn't quite sure what to do at this point, you would probably want to count all the money out loud to let him or her see how you are arriving at the answer. Either way, you or your child should come up with the total of fifty-five cents.

Before we attempt to turn this into a paper and pencil problem, try several more examples similar to the first and see how your child reacts to these. It is important to spend as much time talking out the problem as you need. It is unwise to assume that your child will automatically be able to comprehend the word problem you are demonstrating. Creating a dialogue and leaving room for questions as you proceed is the best way to teach mathematical skills with manipulatives.

Here's another example to try with your child. Once again, using either the manipulative coins or real coins, ask your child to make two groups, one that equals forty cents and another that equals twenty-two cents. You might want to let your child compile these groups without any assistance, unless he or she asks for it. Even if it takes a little time, don't rush it. If your child doesn't ask for help, he or she probably doesn't need it just yet.

Once your child has put together the two groups, ask him or her how much money there is altogether in the two groups. Again, you should not be afraid to demonstrate how you would come up with the answer, but I would recommend encouraging your child to try it first. Even if the answer isn't close, at least making an attempt will demonstrate your child's willingness to learn. Either way, the total for the two groups in this problem should be sixty-two cents.

Here's another example. Ask your child to make two groups of money, one with thirty-three cents and the other with forty-five cents. Once your child has accomplished this task (be sure to watch and check as your child progresses) ask him or her how much money there is together in these two groups.

After counting the two groups, your child should come up with seventy-eight cents. Now that we have explained three examples, ask your child to try the following. Please note that the totals in all of the problems below will be less than one dollar. At this point, we do not want to make the exercise frustrating by going into dollars as well. We explore this concept a bit later.

Ask your child how much money he or she has altogether if he or she has two groups for each of these:

1. **Fifteen cents and twenty-four cents**
2. **Forty-one cents and twenty-five cents**
3. **Fifty-five cents and thirty cents**
4. **Sixty-two cents and eighteen cents**
5. **Eighty-eight cents and eleven cents**
6. **Twenty-four cents and twenty-six cents**
7. **Fifty-one cents and forty-one cents**
8. **Twelve cents and forty cents**
9. **Forty-nine cents and eleven cents**
10. **Seventy-seven cents and nine cents**

Now that we have addressed the skill from a manipulative perspective, let's look at changing it to a paper and pencil skill. Let's take a look at the first problem your child just finished: fifteen cents and twenty-four cents.

On paper, the problem would look like this: 15¢ and 24¢. Let's change these to decimal numbers first: 0.15 and 0.24. Realize that *and* is a key word that means "to add." What we are really looking at is 0.15 + 0.24. You want to explain to your child that when you are adding together two decimal numbers, you must place the decimal points one on top of the other. The problem should look like this:

$$\begin{array}{r} 0.15 \\ + \ 0.24 \\ \hline \end{array}$$

Note that the decimal points are vertically aligned. Once we have the problem set up this way, you simply add. Your child could feel free to use the operational counting sticks in Appendix B or the addition table from Appendix D to complete the problem.

You will want to explain to your child that the decimal point belongs in the same spot in the answer as it is in the problem. In other words, your child will need to bring the decimal point straight down into the answer like this:

$$\begin{array}{r} 0.15 \\ + \ 0.24 \\ \hline . \end{array}$$

After this is done, your child should just add the individual columns to arrive at an answer. When complete, the problem should look like this:

$$\begin{array}{r} 0.15 \\ + \ 0.24 \\ \hline 0.39 \end{array}$$

You should now tell your child when you add fifteen cents and twenty-four cents your total will be thirty-nine cents. Problem solved!

Now let's try the second problem your child tried in the previous exercise: forty-one cents and twenty-five cents.

First you will want to instruct your child to write the numbers as decimal numbers. Second, you will want to tell your child to place the numbers, one on top of the other, and align the decimal points. Once this has been done, direct your child to add the numbers using either the operational counting sticks or the additional table. The problem should look like this when complete:

$$
\begin{array}{r}
0.41 \\
+\ 0.25 \\
\hline
0.66
\end{array}
$$

Once again, you should not hesitate to offer assistance should your child need it, but don't step in prematurely. It's perfectly okay for him or her to make mistakes, as this is part of the learning process. And this is one way he or she will learn that it's okay to make mistakes, it's okay to mess up, it's okay to be wrong. These experiences add to a child's self-esteem and self-confidence, and provide a child with the opportunity to experiment until he or she does come up with the correct response.

Here's one more example you can have your child try with assistance before advancing to several on his or her own. Remember to point out that the decimal points need to be vertically aligned (one on top of the other) or the answer will be incorrect. Ask your child to add forty-eight cents and thirty-one cents.

The key steps you may need to remind your child of are 1) to write each number as a decimal, 2) place the numbers one on top of the other with the decimal points aligned, and 3) add.

When complete, the problem with the answer should look like this:

$$
\begin{array}{r}
0.48 \\
+\ 0.31 \\
\hline
0.79
\end{array}
$$

Now that your child has a better grasp of the concept, have him or her try the following problems. Don't forget to provide assistance, if needed. Ask your child to find the sum for each problem:

1. 22¢ and 45¢
2. 53¢ and 16¢
3. 67¢ and 12¢
4. 88¢ and 10¢
5. 41¢ and 33¢
6. 18¢ and 71¢
7. 26¢ and 22¢
8. 73¢ and 15¢
9. 60¢ and 39¢
10. 30¢ and 20¢

Now that we have addressed the concept of adding decimals, the concept of subtracting decimals is rather easy. Armed with the knowledge of how decimal numbers are added, the subtraction process is exactly the same, except that we subtract the numbers. In other words, 1) change the numbers to decimal numbers, 2) align the decimal points and, 3) subtract. It's that easy. By the way, you will want to introduce the word *difference,* which is the answer to a subtraction problem. So from now on, you will be asking your child to "find the difference" instead of asking him or her to "subtract."

Let's take a look at an example of a problem where we are looking for the difference of two decimal numbers. Find the difference between 69¢ and 23¢.

Remember, step one is to change each number to a decimal number. Therefore, we are going to find the difference between 0.69 and 0.23. Step two tells us to write the decimal numbers one on top of the other, aligning the decimal points.

Now the problem should look like this:

$$\begin{array}{r} 0.69 \\ -\ 0.23 \\ \hline \end{array}$$

Finally, we subtract, and the finished problem should look like this:

$$\begin{array}{r} 0.69 \\ -\ 0.23 \\ \hline 0.46 \end{array}$$

Yes, it's that simple. But once again, we will not be introducing regrouping at this point. It's very important that your child feels completely comfortable with these skills before you introduce regrouping. If you attempt to push too much at any one time, you are likely to cause major confusion. If you approach each skill, one step at a time, the likelihood for success is far greater. And if you think in terms of self-confidence and self-esteem, the pay-off is great when a child succeeds!

Here are several subtraction problems for your child to attempt. Be sure to tell your child that you are looking for the difference between each pair of numbers, and using the operational counting sticks from Appendix B is perfectly acceptable:

1. 78¢ and 12¢
2. 55¢ and 32¢
3. 62¢ and 30¢
4. 85¢ and 51¢
5. 44¢ and 23¢
6. 97¢ and 66¢
7. 37¢ and 15¢
8. 75¢ and 40¢
9. 68¢ and 18¢
10. 59¢ and 27¢

At this point, it might be appropriate to attempt addition and subtraction problems with decimal numbers that involve dollars and cents. Take a look at this one example and see if it might not be the direction you would consider going with your child at this point. Find the sum of $6.22 and $3.37. Remember the steps are *exactly* the same as when you add cent values only.

Step one is to change the dollars and cents to decimal numbers. Step two is to rewrite the numbers, one on top of the other, aligning the decimal points. Step three is to add or subtract, as indicated by the directions.

If done correctly, the problem should look like this:

$$
\begin{array}{r}
6.22 \\
+\ 3.37 \\
\hline
9.59
\end{array}
$$

Therefore, the correct answer to this problem is $9.59. Again, I cannot emphasize enough the value of labeling the answer! Labeling in this case is placing the dollar sign in your answer to clarify your answer.

Here are several problems for your child to try. Remember it is okay for your child to use the operational

counting sticks to assist him or her in solving these problems.
Find each sum:

1. $3.47 and $5.11
2. $4.12 and $4.46
3. $5.10 and $2.49
4. $7.53 and $2.34
5. $1.29 and $3.50

Find each difference:

6. $8.39 and $2.17
7. $6.55 and $1.14
8. $9.58 and $5.33
9. $5.18 and $3.06
10. $7.46 and $4.25

Hopefully by now your child has a better understanding of the concept and usage of decimal numbers. It is most important that your child feel comfortable with what has been accomplished up to this point. You should feel free to devise additional problems should you feel your child would benefit from additional practice.

Throughout this chapter, feel free to allow your child to check his or her answers using a calculator. An electronic calculator is an excellent backup tool as a means of verifying answers.

Children learn by the examples we set for them, so your demonstrations are critical to your child's overall understanding and performance of critical skills. Just remember, keep it simple and have fun!

Here are several challenge problems that you might like to try with your child. Notice that the answers involve carrying into the dollars column or borrowing from the dollars column, so you will need to refer back to chapter 2 should your child experience difficulty with this skill.

1. $9.37 + $5.93
2. $7.71 + $4.46
3. $5.58 + $8.48
4. $13.55 − $8.29
5. $21.35 − $9.46

For additional practice and critical thinking in this area, see chapter 10.

The next logical step after decimals is fractions, primarily because decimals and fractions are both portions of whole numbers. The only difference between the two is that they are represented differently on paper. It is important to understand how closely related to each other they are. The fact that they are both parts of whole numbers is the most important factor here.

CHAPTER nine

Introduction to Fractions

When you enter the realm of fractions, you are entering an area that will open up a whole new world for your child. Up to this point we have addressed whole numbers and have scratched the surface on decimal numbers. Whole numbers are easy for children to understand, in that they are tangible and touchable. The decimal numbers we have explored to this point involve money, something all children can relate to and understand.

Now, fractions are a little more abstract. How so, you ask? How would you explain one-fourth of a dollar to a child without getting into an explanation involving coins? A child would imagine cutting up a one dollar bill and dividing it. So, it's easiest for us to approach this topic with your child by providing tangible examples.

The first question you want to pose is this: What is a fraction? At this point, you need to explain to your child that a fraction is a part of a whole. You also want to explain that a fraction is written in a certain form. The top portion represents the part and the bottom portion represents the whole amount.

Most importantly, you need to discuss with your child the difference between equal and unequal parts. Fractions are *always* made up of equal parts. Therefore, you want to first present this concept to your child before progressing into the details of fractions.

Look at the following illustrations. Ask your child to identify which shapes represent objects divided into equal parts, and which shapes represent objects not divided into equal parts:

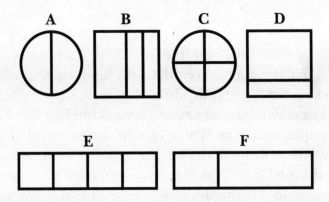

Now that your child has an understanding as to the difference between equal parts and unequal parts, we need to discuss how fractions are written.

Let's look at this example. Let's say that we have four marbles. One marble is blue and three marbles are green. What fraction of the marbles are blue and what fraction of the marbles are green?

This is the way we would write the fractions:

$$\frac{\textbf{1 blue marble}}{\textbf{4 marbles altogether}} \quad \text{or} \quad \frac{1}{4} \quad \text{are blue}$$

$$\frac{\textbf{3 green marbles}}{\textbf{4 marbles altogether}} \quad \text{or} \quad \frac{3}{4} \quad \text{are green}$$

Basically, we have identified the part, as opposed to the whole, in order to establish the relationship in the fraction. Now, let's discuss the figures below:

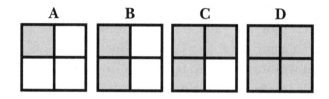

Notice that the boxes are divided into fourths. Box A represents one-fourth, box B represents two-fourths (or one-half), box C represents three-fourths, and box D represents four-fourths (or one whole).

Refer to the Fourths section in Appendix H. You can reproduce these boxes and allow your child to work directly with the copies you have made. After you have done so, ask your child how many parts the box is divided into. The correct response should be four.

Next, explain to your child that each one of the sections or parts represents one-fourth of the box. In terms of the fraction ¼, it is important to explain to your child that the numerator or top part of the fraction represents the part that is shaded in and the denominator or bottom part of the fraction represents how many parts the box or object is divided into. Feel free to use any word or words that will help get your point across. However, I caution you that the more often you use mathematical terminology, the more apt your child will be to retain and use these words appropriately.

At this point, you can do one of several things. Either you can have your child color the four boxes from Appendix H, using a different color for each box or fractional amount that it represents, or you can simply refer to the set of four boxes on page 97. If you are going to have your child color the appropriate sections of each box, be sure that he or she is using four distinctly different colors—one color for each box. Red, blue, yellow and green are good starter colors, so let's use these for our discussion.

You will now want to tell your child that you are going to discuss fractions and what they mean. Tell your child to look at the box he or she has colored blue, and ask him or her how many sections he or she has colored. If you are using the example on the previous page, ask him or her to look at box A. If you are working from the boxes in Appendix H, ask your child to look at the box in the upper left hand corner, also labeled A for clarity. When your child responds "one," tell him or her that this is the top part of the fraction.

Now ask your child how many sections there are altogether in the box. When he or she answers "four," tell him or her that this is the bottom part of the fraction.

Tell your child that the finished fraction should look like this: $\frac{1}{4}$. This means that one-fourth of the box is colored blue, in other words, one out of the four sections of the box is colored blue. The fraction your child has just learned is one-fourth.

Now, using the same technique, ask your child how many sections of the next box are colored red. If you are using the example on page 97, ask your child to look at box B. Your child should answer "two." Now ask your child how many sections there are altogether in the box. He or she should answer "four."

Using the same technique as in the previous example, your child should hopefully see the fraction as two-fourths. Tell your child that the finished fraction should look like this: $^2/_4$. You might also want to explain, at this point, that he or she has actually colored one-half of the box red.

Next, ask your child how many sections are colored in yellow. If you are using the example on page xx, ask him or her to look at box C. He or she should respond "three."

At this point your child should be able to tell you the fraction is three-fourths. If not, a little coaching would be very appropriate. Tell your child that the finished fraction should look like this: $^3/_4$.

Finally, ask your child how many sections are colored in green. When your child responds "four," he or she is likely to be unsure of what to do with this information. The fraction four-fourths maybe confusing. Explain that any fraction with the same number on the top and the bottom is the same as "one." Tell your child that the finished fraction should look like this: $^4/_4$.

Now that we have discussed fourths, let's try another example along the same lines. We are going to look at thirds to see if your child can catch on to what we're explaining about fractions. We are going to do the same thing with thirds that we did with fourths, so use the thirds section in Appendix H for this discussion. Now take a look at the illustrations below:

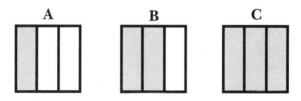

Notice that the boxes are sequential from one-third to three-thirds, left to right. You are going to ask your child to identify each of the fractions based on the part that is shaded in.

For example, in the first illustration on the left, box A, ask your child how many sections are shaded in. Then ask your child how many sections there are total. Remind your child that the numerator is the number of sections shaded in and the denominator is the number of sections altogether.

Your child should be able to identify box A as one-third, or $\frac{1}{3}$. Repeat the same exercise for the second and the third illustrations, boxes B and C, to see if your child can see the pattern. After your child has correctly identified the boxes B and C as two-thirds ($\frac{2}{3}$) and three-thirds ($\frac{3}{3}$), respectively, you may then want to use the manipulatives in Appendix H to continue this exercise.

After you have reproduced the thirds section of Appendix H, you may want to have your child color in the appropriate number of sections that correspond with the value assigned to it. In other words, you may want to ask your child to color in enough of the first illustration under thirds (box A) to make the fraction one-third. If your child follows the direction carefully, he or she should color in only one section of the three divisions in the box.

You could also ask your child to follow the same direction for the second and third illustrations (boxes B and C). Once complete, positive reinforcement always provides the type of feedback necessary for continued success in the areas of self-confidence and self-esteem.

You may also feel free to follow the same path for coloring the halves section in Appendix H. The illustration below can be used to reinforce the concept with your child. Here is an example of one-half and two halves:

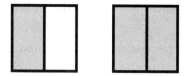

Once your child has the basic understanding of common fractions, including halves, thirds, and fourths, we can then expand our discussion of fractions.

For the following real-life exercise you will need two apples or oranges and a knife to cut them. On the kitchen table, first cut the apple or orange into two equal parts. Emphasize to your child that fractions *always* involve equal parts.

Give one part of the apple to your child and then ask your child what part of the apple he or she is holding. Coaching is fine here. Explain that since you divided the apple into two equal parts, each part is exactly one-half of the apple. Then you should each eat the one half that you have.

With the remaining piece of fruit, you will want to divide it into four equal parts, once again explaining to your child that you are dividing it into four *equal* parts. Then ask your child what part of the fruit he or she will have if you give him or her one part. Then two parts. Then three parts. This exercise is both fun and educational and always of great benefit in explaining the meaning of fractions.

For this next exercise, a bag of jellybeans serves as a fun manipulative your child can eat as you further explain the concept of fractions.

From the bag of jellybeans, count out a group of

twenty jellybeans. The reason I have selected the number twenty is that we are going to be able to discuss fourths, thirds, and halves, in that order, and also allow your child to eat a little bit as we go. Continue reading and you'll see what I mean.

Once you have counted out the twenty jellybeans, ask your child to divide the candy into four equal groups. Provide assistance if necessary, emphasizing that the four groups must have the exact same number of jellybeans *and* you must use *all* the jellybeans.

Now that your child has done so, ask your child how many candies there are in each group. The correct answer is "five." Now tell your child that "five is exactly one-fourth of twenty." You will also want to explain that whenever you are dividing a group into four equal parts, you are actually dividing the entire group into fourths; each part represents one-fourth of the group.

Now that your child has reached this understanding, you can congratulate your child on a job well done. Allow your child to eat five of the jellybeans before proceeding. After your child has eaten five of the candies, ask your child how many jellybeans are left. It is perfectly okay to allow your child to count the leftover jellybeans to arrive at his or her answer.

You may also want to allow your child to use a calculator or the operational counting sticks to check the answer by subtracting five from twenty. Either way, his or her answer should be fifteen.

Now that there are fifteen jellybeans left, ask your child to divide the remaining candies into three equal groups. Explain to your child that the three groups must have exactly the same number of jellybeans in them. When complete, your child should have three groups of five candies. Feel free to assist when necessary.

Next, explain that each one of the three groups represents one-third of all the candy. Two of the groups would represent two-thirds of the jellybeans and all three of the groups would represent three-thirds, or the whole amount of jellybeans.

When complete, congratulate your child for a job well done and allow your child to eat five more of the jellybeans.

Now we are left with ten candies. Finally, you will want to ask your child to divide the remaining candies into two equal groups. Upon completion, there should be two groups, each with five candies in it. You would then want to explain that each group of five represents exactly one-half of the candy. Since there are exactly two groups, each group represents one-half.

By now, hopefully, the concept of fractions is beginning to become more clear to your child. At this point, you can once again congratulate your child on a job well done and allow your child to eat all of the remaining jellybeans! You should feel free to use healthier substitutes if you desire. Using such foods as grapes, oyster crackers, or even sunflower seeds works well with this exercise. For additional practice and critical thinking in this area, see chapter 10.

The next chapter serves as a culmination of all the basic topics presented thus far. It is important that your child learn the appropriate uses for each of the topics. The application of the skills is the most significant, since it demonstrates whether or not your child is understanding these basic skills and can then take this information and utilize it in a problematic setting.

10

Introduction to Problem Solving

This chapter provides additional practice in each of the skill areas that have been addressed in this book. Critical thinking has become the focal direction of contemporary mathematics because it directs children toward the practical uses and applications of math.

Critical thinking allows children to utilize the most basic to the most complex mathematical skills in real-life situations. It affords them ways of seeing why they are learning these fundamental skills and the many benefits to be derived from these skills.

Mathematics is one subject that has a practical side to it, and fortunately children face many life experiences that push them to rely on this knowledge and to use these skills. As adults, we encounter the business world, a carousel of problems waiting to be solved. For those who fail to see the value of math, this world often becomes frustrating and confusing.

Carpeting your living room, fencing in a patio, making a birthday cake, grocery shopping, telling time, and planning a family vacation are just a few of the many situations one encounters that involve mathematical applications. Knowing that the skills and tools to solve these situations are at your fingertips and always available can be very comforting. Hopefully, the bulk of this book has helped your child to start in that positive direction toward understanding and utilizing his or her math skills to begin to solve life's problems.

Now for the problems that begin to scratch the surface and connect your child's basic skills to real life. The problems are divided by section to help connect the concepts in this book together so you can utilize them on a chapter-by-chapter basis. You'll also notice that the level of difficulty increases as you progress through the problems, so pay particular attention to the problems you are giving your child

Remember, again, there is nothing wrong with providing your child with assistance and guidance as he or she is doing a problem. Do your best to lead your child to the answer without actually solving it for him or her. Assistance is one thing, doing the work for your child is quite another.

PROBLEM SOLVING: ADDITION

1. Thomas has a collection of matchbox cars. He has 13 trucks, 21 cars, and 1 fire engine. How many matchbox cars does he have altogether?

2. In the front of the house, Barbara has rose bushes. She has 4 red, 5 pink, 3 yellow, 2 white, and 1 orange. How many rose bushes does she have in all?

3. On the way to school, Brett found 1 nickel, 3 pennies, 2 dimes, and 1 quarter. How many coins did he find altogether?

4. Kurt ate 1 apple on Monday. On Tuesday he ate 1 orange and 1 banana. On Wednesday he ate 2 apples. How much fruit did Kurt eat on those three days?

5. Beth and Mel are keeping track of the mileage they are putting on their car. On Monday they put 17 miles on the car. On Tuesday they put on 14 miles. Wednesday and Thursday together, they put 20 miles on the car. On Friday they only put 7 miles on the car. How many miles did they put on the car that week?

6. Mark works at the mall selling men's clothing on weekends. Last Saturday he sold 15 shirts, 3 ties, and 4 pairs of socks. On Sunday he sold 12 shirts, 7 ties, and 3 pairs of socks. How many items did he sell altogether that weekend?

7. John sells cars at the local used car lot. He sold 5 cars on Saturday and Sunday. He sold 3 cars Monday, 7 cars Tuesday, and 9 cars Wednesday. He did not work on Thursday or Friday. How many cars did he sell over the five-day period?

8. Carlos is planning a trip for this coming weekend. He is packing tomorrow to be sure he is ready to leave on time. He packed 4 shirts, 3 pairs of pants, 2 T-shirts, 1 pair of sweat pants. He also packed 3 pairs of socks. How many articles of clothing did he pack altogether?

9. Melissa does 2 loads of laundry on Saturday, 2 loads on Sunday, and 1 load each day for the rest of the week. How many loads of laundry does Melissa do for her family each week?

10. Alex loves to collect baseball cards. Last year he bought 31 new baseball cards. He already had 41 cards in his collection. He plans to buy another package of 20 baseball cards. How many baseball cards will he have in his collection altogether?

PROBLEM SOLVING: SUBTRACTION

1. Karen had 8 different pairs of earrings. She went on a trip and lost 2 pairs. How many pairs does she now have left?

2. Gloria loves to paint landscapes for her friends. Last year she painted 16 paintings. She gave 3 away to her friends and sold 1. How many paintings does Gloria have left?

3. Beth took her daughters to the park for the afternoon. Each of her two daughters brought 4 toys along. Each daughter lost 1 toy at the park. How many toys did Beth's daughters bring home from the park altogether?

4. Steve went to the batting cage to practice hitting baseballs. The pitching machine threw 25 baseballs altogether. Steve hit 17 of the baseballs. How many baseballs did he miss?

5. Abbie bought a book of stamps at the post office. There are 25 stamps in the book she purchased. She used 8 stamps to mail letters. How many stamps does Abbie have left in the book?

6. The used car lot has 57 cars for sale. There is a sale planned for the weekend. If the salespeople sell 23 cars during the sale, how many cars will be left?

7. Susan bought a package of tulip bulbs to plant in her garden. There were 40 bulbs in the package. She planted 20 bulbs. How many bulbs are left in the package?

8. Mark has 24 baseball trading cards. John has 35 baseball trading cards. They decided to put their cards together. Then they traded 22 cards. How many cards did they have left?

9. David sold 30 CDs at his garage sale. He originally had 76 CDs. How many does he now have left?

10. There are 97 biographies at the library. On Saturday 23 biographies were checked out. On Sunday 21 biographies were checked out. How many biographies are still on the shelf in the library?

PROBLEM SOLVING: MULTIPLICATION

1. Jeff runs 5 miles each day. How many miles will Jeff run on Friday, Saturday, and Sunday together?

2. Barbara saves pennies in jars. She has 7 jars. There are 9 pennies in each jar. How many pennies does she have altogether?

3. Sid manages the local little league team. He stores baseball equipment in his van. He has 2 bats for each player on the team. There are 13 players on the team. How many baseball bats does Sid have in his van?

4. Elliot works at the hardware store. He sees exactly 11 customers each day. How many customers does he see from Monday through Friday?

5. Debbie has roses, tulips, mums, daffodils, and lilacs in her garden. She has 10 of each plant. How many flowering plants does she have altogether?

6. Mr. Hayes is taking his students on a field trip. He teaches grades 6, 7, and 8. He takes 20 students from each class. How many students did he take on the trip altogether?

7. Kennedy High School has 8 buses. Each bus seats 60 students. How many students altogether can the buses transport at one time?

8. Mrs. Williams teaches 5 classes of Algebra a day. She has 32 students in each class. How many students does Mrs. Williams teach altogether?

9. Aaron learns 20 new vocabulary words in his English class each week. There are 9 weeks in a grading period. How many new vocabulary words will Aaron learn in two grading periods?

10. Charlotte runs a dog kennel. She trains collies, retrievers, labradors, and springer spaniels. She had 20 of each breed in her kennel. She sold 5 of each breed. How many dogs does she have in the kennel altogether now?

PROBLEM SOLVING: DIVISION

1. Phyllis has a collection of 20 antique buttons. She has 5 containers to put the buttons into. She wants to put the same number of buttons into each container. How many should go into each container?

2. Michael paints houses. He has 40 gallons of paint in stock. Each paint can holds 2 gallons. How many paint cans does Michael have altogether?

3.   Dr. Jaffe sees 35 patients each work week. (One work week = five days.) He sees the same number of patients each day. How many patients does Dr. Jaffe see in one day?

4.   Miss Boras bought 48 jumbo crayons for her class. She has enough to give 2 crayons to each student. How many students does she have altogether?

5.   Patrick has 28 shoes in his closet. There are 2 shoes in each pair. How many pairs of shoes does Patrick have in his closet?

6.   Betty has roses in her garden. Each plant has 3 flowers on it. She counted 36 flowers this morning. How many rose bushes does she have in her garden?

7.   Barney loves to play with his computer. He has computer games, educational programs, and business software. He has the same number of programs in each category. He has a total of 30 programs. How many computer games does Barney have?

8.   Anthony works at the zoo. He is in charge of the reptile house. There are 88 reptiles altogether in the reptile house. There are 8 different reptile cages. There are the same number of reptiles in each cage. How many reptiles are in each cage?

9.   Mr. Lindbergh has 80 tubes of acrylic paint. He has 8 plastic containers to hold the paint. He wants to put the same number of tubes of paint into each container. How many tubes of acrylic paint should he put into each plastic container?

10. Mr. Evans is responsible for ordering all the office supplies for his office. Each cabinet in the office

stock room will hold 20 packages of computer paper. When the cabinets are full, there are 100 packages of computer paper. How many cabinets hold computer paper?

PROBLEM SOLVING: MONEY

1. Marilyn has 37¢ in her wallet. She has exactly 4 coins. What coins does Marilyn have in her wallet?

2. Alex has 22¢ in his pocket. Mark has 35¢ in his pocket. How much money do they have together?

3. Melissa went to the store to buy a small carton of milk. She has 89¢ in her purse. The milk costs 67¢. After she pays for the milk, How much money will Melissa have left?

4. Stuart has 5 jars with pennies in them. There are 10 pennies in each jar. How many pennies does Stuart have altogether?

5. Vincent has $5.33 in his piggy bank. Jason has $8.59 in his piggy bank. Who has more money in his bank? How much more?

PROBLEM SOLVING: TIME

1. Amy needs to be at school by 8:00 A.M. She wakes up at 7:00 A.M. How much time does Amy have to get ready and get to school?

2. Ryan looks at his wristwatch. The minute hand is on the 6. The hour hand is on the 4. What time is it?

3. Douglas leaves the office at 5:00 P.M. It takes him one and one-half hours to drive home in rush hour traffic. What time should Douglas expect to get home?

4. Andrew leaves work to take a lunch break. He leaves the office at 12:30 P.M. He has 45 minutes for lunch. What time must he be back at work?

5. Linda wants to go shopping. She is planning to leave home at 10:00 A.M. She needs to be home by 2:30 P.M. How much time does she have to shop?

PROBLEM SOLVING: CALENDARS

1. The 15th of June is on a Saturday. What day of the week is the 25th day of June? The 1st day of June? The last day of June?

2. Anthony has to turn a science project in on Friday. Today is Tuesday. How many days does Anthony have left to finish this project?

3. Martin is going to take a two-week vacation from work. He leaves on November 5th. What day should he expect to return from his vacation?

4. Adrienne is going to take a three-week vacation from work. How many days vacation is three weeks?

5. Carla is looking forward to summer vacation from school this year. She does not have to go to school in July or August. How many days of summer vacation will Carla have?

PROBLEM SOLVING: DECIMALS

1. Vinnie has eighty-six cents in his pocket and Roy has thirty-nine cents in his pocket. Write these numbers as decimal numbers.

2. Eric has $4.59 in his bank. He also has $2.30 in his wallet. How much money does Eric have altogether?

3. Tony has $9.66 in his wallet. Keith has $7.43 in his wallet. Who has more money in his wallet, Tony or Keith? How much more?

4. Andre and his brother, Matt, are saving up their allowances to buy a remote control car. The car costs $39.95. Andre has $16.37. Matt has $21.22. If they put their money together, do they have enough to buy it?

5. Ben has two jars with coins in them. One jar has $1.22 and the other jar has $2.16. John has one jar with $3.77. Who has more money, Ben or John? How much more?

PROBLEM SOLVING: FRACTIONS

1. Marsha cut 3 apples into halves. She gave 1 to her son and 1 to her daughter. She and her husband also had 1 each. How many halves were left?

2. Lance cut a pizza to share with his friends. He gave $\frac{1}{3}$ of the pizza to Bill. He gave $\frac{1}{4}$ of the pizza to Tom. Did he give a larger share to Bill or to Tom?

3. Bob has a collection of 10 model airplanes. Three of these airplanes are jets. What fraction of his airplanes are jets?

4. Alan and Alisa both have the same size jars. They split a bag of candy. Alan filled one-half of his jar. Alisa filled two-thirds of her jar. Who has more candy, Alan or Alisa?

5. Evan's car has ¾ of a tank of gas. Jeff's car has ½ of a tank of gas. Both tanks hold the same amount of gas. Whose car has more gas in it?

CHAPTER
eleven

Challenges

When you and your child have surpassed the limits explored in the previous chapters, you might want to explore further challenges that extend beyond the topics presented thus far. Although this chapter applies to all children, the gifted child will be more adept at taking basic skills and applying them to situations that are a step beyond initial learning.

Let's start with the basic operations of adding and subtracting whole numbers. Chapter 2 addresses these operations with operational counting sticks and only at a most basic level. Here are a series of problems that go slightly beyond that level. With very little direction and instruction, see if your child can attack them.

ADDITION AND SUBTRACTION OF WHOLE NUMBERS

1. 25,628 + 14,995
2. 237,991 + 19,575

3. 509,278 + 100,005
4. 57,772 – 18,449
5. 109,233 – 88,457
6. 500,278 – 327,659
7. 300,000 – 166,923

Chapter 3 discusses basic multiplication, but only to the point where we multiply a two-digit number by a one-digit number. What happens when we multiply a two-digit number by another two-digit number or a three-digit number by a two- or three-digit number? The process is a little more involved, but no doubt one where a more gifted child is likely to see the pattern developing in multiplication. Now would be an appropriate time to discuss the placement of zeros in an answer when the number of digits in the answer exceeds four. Here is another series of problems that addresses this particular type of longer multiplication problem.

MULTIPLICATION OF WHOLE NUMBERS

1.   47 × 34
2.   68 × 81
3.   59 × 20
4.   263 × 52
5.   109 × 48
6.   745 × 70
7.   811 × 103
8.   593 × 476
9. 1293 × 562
10. 2744 × 2913

Division is another story altogether—one that chapter 4 covers. When the divisor you are dealing with is a single digit it's one thing, but when the divisors become two and even three digits, the problem's complexity increases drastically. Assistance will probably be in order for this next series of problems in that your child will probably have a difficult time getting started. Limit your assistance, if possible, since the purpose of this chapter is to challenge. The less assistance, the greater the challenge. You will need to tell your child that some of these problems will have remainders, while others will not.

DIVISION OF WHOLE NUMBERS

1. $2256 \div 47$
2. $1007 \div 19$
3. $14,375 \div 23$
4. $40,052 \div 68$
5. $1897 \div 30$
6. $2003 \div 58$
7. $26,524 \div 19$
8. $73,809 \div 36$

Chapter 5 presents the concept of money with the attitude that this is something everyone most readily adjusts to. It is a concept even the smallest child learns at a very young age. Children seem to enjoy almost any problem based upon the use of money. We discuss operations with money in chapter 8, but we do not get into multiplying or dividing with money and what you do when you have a remainder in a situation such as this. Rounding off to the nearest penny is new unchartered territory that may take a little time to explain, but will be well worth the time in exercises such as these. For example, you cannot have the answer $26.2565. You must round up or down to the nearest cent, so your answer should actually be $26.26.

OPERATIONS WITH MONEY

1. $4.27 × 0.77
2. $6.25 × 0.15
3. $18.27 × 0.05
4. $26.94 × 2.26
5. $8.25 ÷ 5.3
6. $6.63 ÷ 1.4
7. $27.88 ÷ 0.55
8. $300.00 ÷ 2.7

Chapter 9 makes clear that fractions are a unique unit of math. The rules and regulations that guide operations with fractions apply to no other parts of math. Knowing how to put fractions in their lowest terms, finding equivalent fractions, or even operating with fractions is so completely different from other mathematical functions that it practically defies definition. This challenge section on fractions encompasses challenge-oriented problems with almost every facet of fractions, therefore assistance and guidance will be necessary to start your child off with each.

FRACTIONS IN LOWEST TERMS

1. $4/12$
2. $6/9$
3. $8/16$
4. $9/12$
5. $10/50$
6. $12/48$
7. $24/36$
8. $16/96$

FINDING EQUIVALENT FRACTIONS

1. $\dfrac{5}{10} = \dfrac{?}{6}$

2. $\dfrac{8}{20} = \dfrac{?}{15}$

3. $\dfrac{9}{12} = \dfrac{?}{8}$

4. $\dfrac{10}{15} = \dfrac{?}{12}$

5. $\dfrac{12}{15} - \dfrac{?}{20}$

6. $\dfrac{24}{36} = \dfrac{?}{3}$

OPERATIONS WITH FRACTIONS

1. $2/5 + 2/5$
2. $1/4 + 3/8$
3. $7/10 + 5/6$
4. $7/8 - 3/8$
5. $4/5 - 1/3$

6. $9/10 - 2/3$
7. $1/4 \times 1/2$
8. $2/5 \times 5/8$
9. $2/3 \times 9/15$

Now that we have explored the serious side of math we don't want your child to leave this experience thinking that math is all hard work and not really fun and games when it actually can be. The final chapter of this book looks at the *fun* side of math. Hopefully we can end this experience on a positive note and leave your child with the feeling that math truly can be a great deal of fun!

CHAPTER
twelve

Puzzles and Games

Math has always been a subject that lends itself to a variety of formats. The pencil and paper, computational aspect is the one most people are familiar with. There is also the calculator, problem-solving aspect that uses basic computational skills to solve real-life problems. Depending on your source, some call it concepts, some call it application, and still others call it problem solving. No matter what you call it, the end result should always be the same; the perfect solution to a real-life problem.

One aspect of math that is usually overlooked is the game/puzzle format. Here we have an opportunity to turn learning into fun. We can take some of the drudgery out of learning mathematics and bring some of the fun back into it just by changing the way it is presented.

This chapter is designed to provide you with a variety of strategies to present various mathematical skills *and* allow you and your child to have a lot of fun at the same time.

Each game or puzzle is preceded by an explanation of the skill(s) involved, how to play, and the expected outcome.

Be sure to provide some type of reward for the successful completion of each game. The reward does not necessarily have to be candy. Use your imagination to provide these rewards, but don't underestimate their importance. They will provide a great deal of positive reinforcement, which is, of course, the best way for a child to learn.

Hopefully, this chapter will shed some light on new ways to explore the possibilities and the realities of math while having fun at the same time!

THE BASIC COUNTING BOARD GAME

This particular board game is designed to assist your child with learning to count. The board will cover counting from one through twenty-nine and with the numbers clearly written on the game board it is as easy as 1,2,3 to play.

To play, you will need the board, one die, and two markers. The game is designed for two people. Each person rolls the die to see who goes first. The person who rolls the highest number goes first. You may even want to have your child color the board to make it more cheerful.

Each player takes one turn and rolls the die, moving his or her marker the number of spaces indicated on the face of the die. The person who gets to the finish first wins. Be sure you and your child count the numbers *out loud* as you move through the board to reinforce counting skills.

Your child's basic counting skills should improve after several plays of this game. You might even want to test your child's ability to count without looking at the board after you have played the game several times.

You can continue using this game as a measure of how well your child adapts to basic counting skills.

BASIC COUNTING
BOARD GAME

Start
Here

1		7	8	9	10
2		6			11
3	4	5			12
					13
19	18	17	16	15	14
20					
21		25	26	27	28
22	23	24			29

Finish
Here

TALLYING MEASURES

This game utilizes a child's ability to use simple measurements of various household items.

This game can be played by two to five players. Each player needs either a ruler or a tape measure, a pencil, a pad of paper, and a calculator.

Each person has exactly three minutes to bring five household objects to the kitchen table. Once all players are at the table, each measures the length (the longest measure) of each object. Each measure is then written down on the player's own pad of paper. When the players have finished measuring and writing down the measurements, each then uses a calculator to total (or tally) the measures.

The player with the largest tally wins. You should have all players use the same unit of measure (all inches or all centimeters) to ensure accuracy. You might even want to take turns double-checking the other's answers to ensure accuracy.

COMPUTING WITH CARDS

A simple deck of playing cards can be a most useful and creative tool in math. The number of players in the game is limitless, however, the most fun is had when played by two or three players. Most card games use one or more math skills anyway, but what we are going to do specifically targets a child's basic computational skills and strengthens these skills through repetitive play.

"Computing with Cards" is a game that can be used to target any or all of a child's basic computational skills. You can direct the game to target adding, subtracting, multiplying, or dividing or any combination thereof.

To target addition, each person draws five cards, totals them, and the winner of the round is the player with the highest total. Each picture card counts as ten points. Reshuffle when you have exhausted the deck. You determine whether five or ten rounds constitute a game.

To target subtraction, each player draws one card. The players with the highest and the lowest cards find the difference between the cards. The points (or difference) are awarded to the person who originally had the highest card. The first player to reach fifty points or one hundred points wins.

To target multiplication, each player is dealt ten cards facedown. One at a time, each player selects two of his or her opponent's cards. The opponent turns his or her two cards over and multiplies the two numbers (all picture cards count as ten). The opponent then writes down the answer to the multiplication problem. When all players have exhausted their cards, all players tally their answers. The person with the highest tally wins. You could also add excitement if you choose to penalize each player for any and all wrong answers. You could make it an automatic five-point deduction for every incorrect answer.

To target division, each player is dealt an equal portion of the deck. The entire deck is dealt with all leftover cards placed on the side and disqualified. One at a time, each player selects two of his or her opponent's cards to see if one card cannot be divided evenly into another. If the cards can, the opponent then divides the two and writes down the answer. If the two cards *cannot* be divided, another card is selected and so on until two of the cards can be divided evenly.

The next player follows suit. This goes on until all cards have been exhausted. Each player then tallies his or her answers (or quotients) and the player with the most points wins.

IT'S ONLY MONEY

There's a very simple game with money that helps reinforce the individual values of various coins and a child's ability to separate and differentiate between the different coins.

This money game should be played by at least two players. Each player should be given five of each of the following coins: pennies, nickels, dimes, and quarters.

Each player takes a turn selecting an amount of money greater than five cents and less than one dollar. Each player tries to find as many ways as possible to "put together" that amount with the coins given. All coins can be used more than once. Points should be awarded based on the number of different combinations each player can come up with.

Another way of awarding points for this game would be to give a limited amount of time to complete the task.

You can select the number of rounds to play before the game is complete or you could decide that the first person to get a certain number of points wins. You decide!

DAYS, WEEKS, MONTHS

The following board game is designed to provide additional reinforcement on days, weeks, and months. Here's how the game works: Each player (from two to four) starts with four markers. All players start from either box 1, 2, 3, or 4. The object of this game is to be the first to get all four markers into the home boxes in the center of the board. You will need one die and to cut out the playing cards that appear on page 131.

Each player rolls the die once to determine playing order. The first player moves one marker to box A. He or she then rolls the die. His or her opponent will then ask the question from card A that corresponds to the roll of the die. If the player answers the question correctly, he or she then advances to box B and rolls the die again. The same player keeps moving forward until he or she incorrectly answers a question. When he or she answers a question incorrectly, it then becomes the next player's turn.

The only penalty for an incorrect answer is that the turn ends at that time. The first person to move all four markers into home wins. You can only enter home directly from box F.

Feel free to alter rules that fit your style of playing and the level of difficulty your child can handle. You can also devise your own calendar questions. Just remember to keep it fun. The fun experiences are the ones your child will want most to replay. The best part is that your child will be learning at the same time he or she is playing!

DAYS, WEEKS, MONTHS
A CALENDAR BOARD GAME

A	1			2	A
B					B
C		HOME			C
D	E	F	F	E	D
C		HOME			C
B					B
A	4			3	A

DAYS, WEEKS, MONTHS
BOARD GAME CARDS

CARD A

1. How many days in two weeks?
2. What day comes after Monday?
3. How many hours in two days?
4. How many days in September?
5. How many months in one year?
6. What day comes before Thursday?

CARD B

1. What day comes after Friday?
2. How many days in August?
3. How many months in two years?
4. What day comes before Sunday?
5. How many days in December?
6. How many hours in one day?

CARD C

1. What day comes after Tuesday?
2. How many days in May?
3. How many days in one week?
4. How many weeks in one month?
5. How many weeks in February?
6. What day comes before Friday?

CARD D

1. How many days in January?
2. What day comes after Sunday?
3. How many days in October?
4. How many days in three weeks?
5. What day comes before Wednesday?
6. How many days in June?

CARD E

1. How many days in one year?
2. How many days n November?
3. What day comes after Thursday?
4. How many days in two weeks?
5. What day comes before Monday?
6. What year is this?

CARD F

1. How many days in February?
2. What day comes after Wednesday?
3. How many days in July?
4. What year is next year?
5. How many days in four weeks?
6. What day comes before Thursday?

It seems the best way to end this chapter is to finish with a cross number puzzle. Similar to a crossword puzzle, it calls on all of the child's skills to complete. Just as in a crossword puzzle, there is exactly one letter or number per box. The rest of it is really quite simple.

You may want to help your child get started by trying either one item across or one item down, or even both. Your child will begin to get the idea and have a ball in the meantime.

CROSS NUMBER PUZZLE
A CROSSWORD PUZZLE FOR NUMBERS

CROSS NUMBER CLUES

ACROSS	DOWN
1. 9×3	1. 5×4
2. $298 + 2$	2. $39 - 4$
3. $30 \div 2$	3. $110 + 2$
4. 7×6	4. 7×7
5. $15 + 10$	6. The number of cards in one deck.
9. $100 + 100$	
10. The number of pennies in one dollar.	7. $121 - 20$

With all the material presented thus far, a child might find it difficult to believe that this is just the beginning of a long math experience! We have just begun to interest and excite a young mind by whetting the appetite and offering some sound beginnings to a field that will unfold in years to come. I hope this experience has served as a motivational and practical tool to getting your child started in what is likely to be a challenging and exciting future in the field of mathematics.

Shapes and Sizes

On this and the next page you will find four of each of the following shapes: squares, circles, rectangles, ovals, and triangles. You will want to photocopy and enlarge these pages, then color and cut out at least four of each shape and size for use with the section on patterns. You might even want to trace these onto cardboard to add to the durability of the shapes.

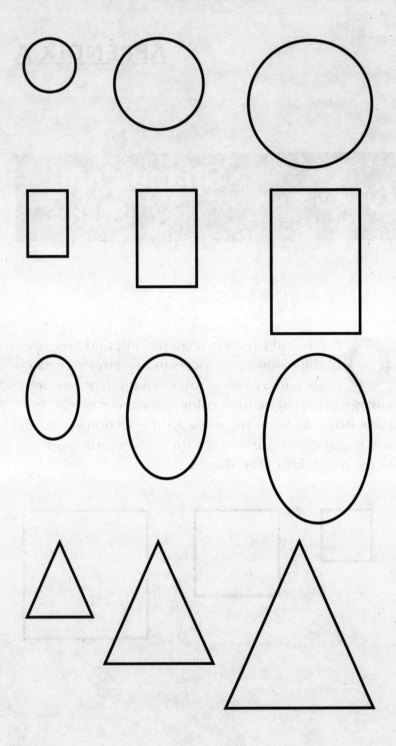

Operational
Counting Sticks

The counting sticks on the next page will need to be photocopied, enlarged, and cut out. For more durable counting sticks, you might want to trace these onto cardboard. Have your child color them with crayons following this color scheme:

A - Brown	B - Blue	C - Pink	D - Yellow
E - Silver	F - Orange	G - Green	H - Black
J - Gold	K - Red		

The number value for each color stick is listed below. You might want to print this number directly on the stick to help reinforce skills to be taught with these sticks:

A - 1	B - 2	C - 3	D - 4
E - 5	F - 6	G - 7	H - 8
J - 9	K - 10		

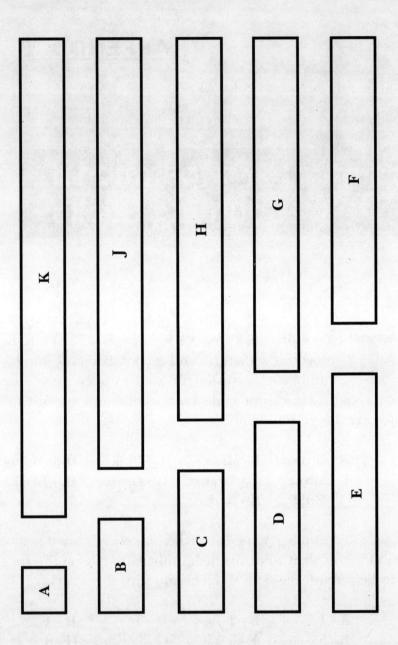

APPENDIX C

Addition/Multiplication Table

On the next page is a multiplication table you can complete with your child. Use the operational counting sticks in Appendix B to complete the table for use with chapter 3, Learning to Multiply. You may want to complete this activity with your child over a period of several days since it could become rather tedious to try and complete this table in one day. Then allow your child to use this table for the second part of chapter 3 when you are teaching your child to multiply a two-digit number by a one-digit number. This will help speed up the computation process and make the entire operation more fun.

Special Note: You might want to consider using this as an addition table if your child is experiencing difficulty in retaining his or her basic addition skills. You could simply photocopy the table and change the multiplication symbol to an addition symbol for this purpose.

ADDITION/MULTIPLICATION TABLE

+/x	1	2	3	4	5	6	7	8	9	10
1										
2										
3										
4										
5										
6										
7										
8										
9										
10										

Coins

You should use the coins on the next page instead of real coins at first to provide a more hands-on experience for your child. First photocopy these onto another piece of paper. Then have your child cut them out and color them to help differentiate between the coin values. For more durable coins, you might want to trace the coins onto cardboard. You will want your child to color the pennies brown, the nickels silver, the dimes red, and the quarters blue. This will help your child visually separate the coins.

Cutting out and coloring the coins will also provide you with the opportunity to discuss the different values of the coins with your child. The penny and the nickel have been designed to be colored close to the color of the actual coin. You should make this point to your child. The dime and the quarter should not be colored silver in that it would be difficult for your child to visually separate all coins.

Once the cutting and the coloring of coins is complete, you will probably want to bring out real coins to show your child how they compare in size, and with the penny and the nickel, in color.

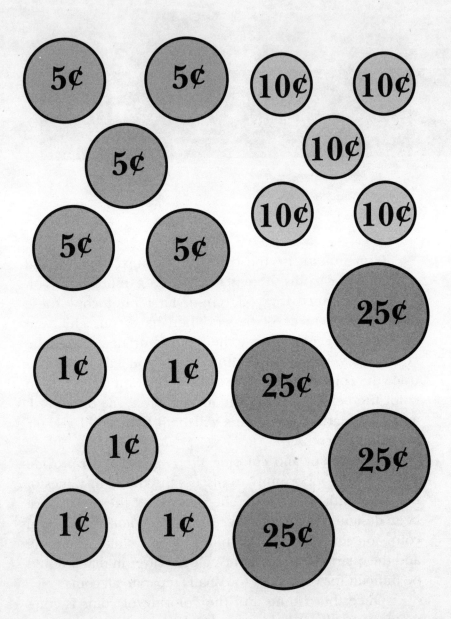

Table of Math Problems

You might want to use the following table of problems to enhance your child's ability in the areas of addition, subtraction, multiplication, and division. If you repeat the problems with your child frequently, he or she is likely to retain them more rapidly. This is certainly one way to increase your child's speed and accuracy in basic skills.

ADDITION	SUBTRACTION	MULTIPLICATION	DIVISION
Column A	Column B	Column C	Column D
4 + 5	8 − 2	3 × 5	8 ÷ 4
2 + 7	9 − 4	2 × 1	9 ÷ 3
1 + 6	5 − 1	4 × 2	2 ÷ 1
3 + 3	4 − 2	1 × 9	10 ÷ 2
0 + 5	2 − 1	3 × 3	6 ÷ 3
9 + 1	7 − 5	8 × 1	8 ÷ 2
8 + 0	6 − 0	2 × 2	7 ÷ 1
5 + 3	5 − 2	1 × 6	4 ÷ 2
1 + 7	8 − 5	3 × 2	6 ÷ 2
2 + 6	9 − 3	5 × 2	10 ÷ 5

A Clock with Moveable Hands

After photocopying and enlarging, color and cut out the clock and hands on the next page. After you have cut them out, you can attach the hands to the clock with a clasp fastened through the center. You might even want to mount this clock on cardboard to make it more durable. Please note that the hands are marked with the words *hours* and *minutes* to help your child understand that the two hands perform separate functions.

To assist your child with telling time, you will want to position the hands on the clock in numerous ways to represent different times. This should assist you in teaching the concept of telling time.

Mark off the minutes on the face of the clock to help teach minutes. You will need to make four marks between each pair of numbers on the face of the clock and explain to your child that there are five minutes between each pair of numbers on the clock.

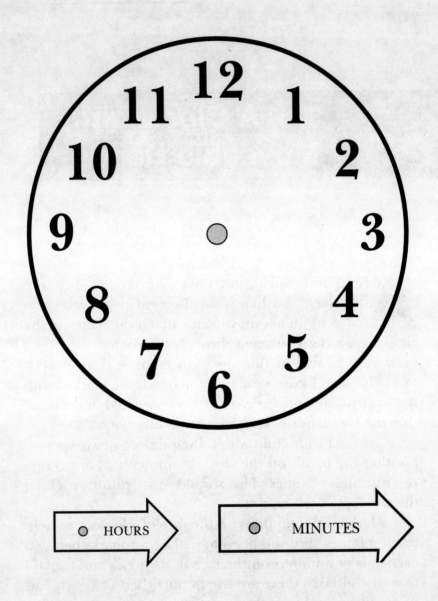

Calendars

On the next page is a generic one-month calendar. It is designed to allow you to fill in your own month and dates so you can tailor it to your needs. You will probably want to make an enlarged set of twelve so you can make a one-year calendar and mark in all the holidays, family birthdays, and other important dates as a way to keep your child posted on all important upcoming dates.

I also encourage you to have your child color in the calendar days so as to make it a hands-on activity.

Feel free to use your own creativity to assist your child in the creation of your own twelve-month calendar.

MONTH: _____

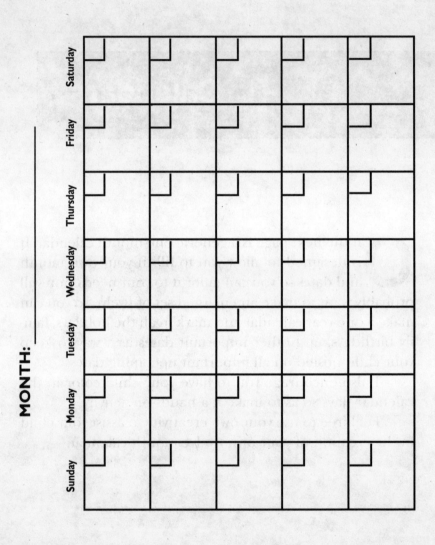

Sunday	Monday	Tuesday	Wednesday	Thursday	Friday	Saturday

Fractions

The next several pages contain examples of fractions representing fourths, thirds, and halves. These should be used when explaining fractions to your child. They correlate with chapter 9. Feel free to have your child color and cut out these figures to better understand fractions.

You will want to photocopy them and have your child color them in accordance with the values assigned to them. For instance, the first example, labeled one-fourth (box A) should only have one of the four sections colored in. Have your child use the color assigned to each box. The idea is to help your child learn the fractional values as he or she cuts and colors the shapes. Hands-on is the key to learning here.

FOURTHS

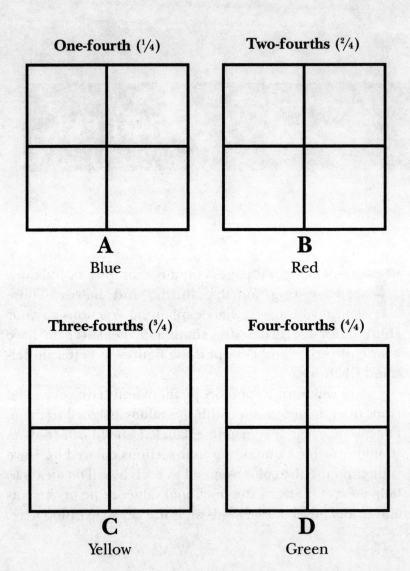

One-fourth (¹⁄₄)

A

Blue

Two-fourths (²⁄₄)

B

Red

Three-fourths (³⁄₄)

C

Yellow

Four-fourths (⁴⁄₄)

D

Green

HALVES

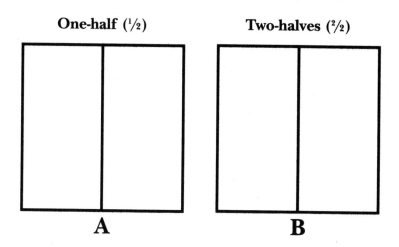

One-half ($\frac{1}{2}$)　　　　　Two-halves ($\frac{2}{2}$)

A　　　　　　　B

THIRDS

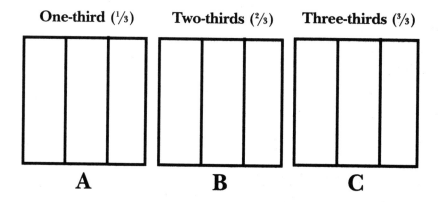

One-third ($\frac{1}{3}$)　　Two-thirds ($\frac{2}{3}$)　　Three-thirds ($\frac{3}{3}$)

A　　　　　B　　　　　C

HALVES

One-half (½) Two-halves (²⁄₂)

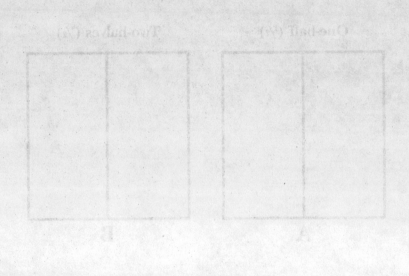

A   B

THIRDS

One-third (⅓) Two-thirds (⅔) Three-thirds (³⁄₃)

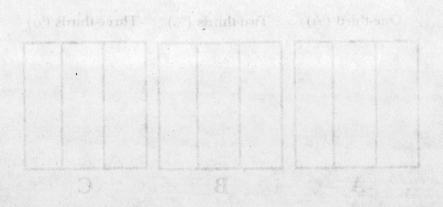

A   B   C

Answer Key

CHAPTER 2: LEARNING TO ADD AND SUBTRACT

page 28	page 33	page 35	page 36	page 37
1. 6	1. 5	1. 87	1. 62	1. 6418
2. 4	2. 2	2. 77	2. 52	2. 3722
3. 4	3. 5	3. 78	3. 31	3. 9102
4. 8	4. 2	4. 87	4. 33	4. 348
5. 7	5. 0	5. 88	5. 21	5. 556
		6. 63	6. 60	
		7. 97	7. 22	
		8. 59	8. 22	
		9. 79	9. 53	
		10. 77	10. 11	

CHAPTER 3: LEARNING TO MULTIPLY

page 41	page 44	page 47	page 50	page 51
1. 6	1. 6	1. 88	1. 152	1. 2166
2. 8	2. 10	2. 39	2. 96	2. 3300
3. 12	3. 7	3. 68	3. 120	3. 4316
4. 3	4. 9	4. 47	4. 301	4. 760
5. 4	5. 8	5. 55	5. 81	5. 4345
6. 10	6. 4	6. 48	6. 38	
7. 5	7. 5	7. 123	7. 165	
8. 6	8. 4	8. 59	8. 184	
9. 8	9. 1	9. 124	9. 416	
10. 1	10. 10	10. 155	10. 150	

CHAPTER 4: LEARNING TO DIVIDE

page 55	page 56
1. 3	1. 2R2
2. 3	2. 4R1
3. 1	3. 2R2
4. 2	4. 2R1
5. 4	5. 2R1
6. 5	6. 2R1
7. 3	7. 1R3
8. 2	8. 3R1
9. 5	9. 1R4
10. 2	10. 1R2

CHAPTER 6: A MATTER OF TIME

page 73	page 74
1. 1 hour 15 minutes	1. 180
2. 2 hours 45 minutes	2. 60
3. 1 hour 30 minutes	3. 2
4. 2 hours 45 minutes	4. 1
5. 2 hours 40 minutes	5. 180
6. 2 hours 30 minutes	6. 3
7. 1 hour 45 minutes	7. 120
8. 2 hours 55 minutes	8. 300
9. 3 hours 35 minutes	9. 1
10. 2 hours 30 minutes	10. 3600

CHAPTER 7: MONTH BY MONTH

page 79	page 80	page 82
1. 9 days	1. - 13.	1. 5
2. 3 days	depends	2. Sunday
3. 12 days	on year	3. Tuesday
4. 7 days		4. Saturday, March 12
5. 11 days		5. Thursday
6. 9 days		6. Monday, March 21
7. 12 days		7. 4
8. 10 days		8. Thursday
9. 14 days		9. Friday
10. 9 days		10. Monday, March 7

CHAPTER 8: INTRODUCTION TO DECIMALS

page 83	page 87	page 90
1. 0.89	1. 39¢	1. 67¢
2. 0.44	2. 66¢	2. 69¢
3. 0.99	3. 85¢	3. 79¢
4. 0.50	4. 80¢	4. 98¢
5. 0.26	5. 99¢	5. 74¢
6. 1.10	6. 50¢	6. 89¢
7. 4.39	7. 92¢	7. 48¢
8. 8.15	8. 52¢	8. 88¢
9. 11.60	9. 60¢	9. 99¢
10. 21.21	10. 86¢	10. 50¢

page 92	page 93	page 94
1. 66¢	1. $8.58	1. $15.30
2. 23¢	2. $8.58	2. $12.17
3. 32¢	3. $7.59	3. $14.06
4. 34¢	4. $9.87	4. $5.26
5. 21¢	5. $4.79	5. $11.89
6. 31¢	6. $6.22	
7. 22¢	7. $5.41	
8. 35¢	8. $4.25	
9. 50¢	9. $2.12	
10. 32¢	10. $3.21	

CHAPTER 10: INTRODUCTION TO PROBLEM SOLVING

page 106

Addition

1. 35 cars
2. 15 bushes
3. 7 coins
4. 5 pieces
5. 58 miles
6. 44 items
7. 24 cars
8. 13 articles
9. 9 loads
10. 92 cards

page 108

Subtraction

1. 6 pair
2. 12 paintings
3. 6 toys
4. 8 baseballs
5. 17 stamps
6. 34 cars
7. 20 bulbs
8. 37 cards
9. 46 CDs
10. 53 bios

page 109

Multiplication

1. 15 miles
2. 63 pennies
3. 26 bats
4. 55 customers
5. 50 plants
6. 60 students
7. 480 students
8. 160 students
9. 360 words
10. 60 dogs

page 110

Division

1. 4 buttons
2. 20 cans
3. 7 patients
4. 24 students
5. 14 pair
6. 12 bushes
7. 10 games
8. 11 reptiles
9. 10 tubes
10. 5 cabinets

page 112

Money

1. 1 quarter
   dime
   pennies
2. 59¢
3. 22¢
4. 50 pennies
5. Jason, $3.26

page 112

Time

1. 1 hour
2. 4:30
3. 6:30 P.M.
4. 1:15 P.M.
5. 4 hours and
   30 minutes

page 113

Calendars

1. Tuesday,
   Saturday,
   Sunday
2. 3 days
3. November 19
4. 21 days
5. 62 days

page 114

Decimals

1. 0.86, 0.39
2. $6.89
3. Tony, $2.23
4. No
5. John, 39¢

page 114

Fractions

1. 2 halves
2. Bill
3. $^3/_{10}$
4. Alisa
5. Evan

CHAPTER 11: CHALLENGES

page 117

Adding/Subtracting Whole Numbers

1. 40,623
2. 257,566
3. 609,283
4. 39,323
5. 20,766
6. 172,619
7. 133,077

page 118

Multiply Whole Numbers

1. 1598
2. 5508
3. 1180
4. 13,676
5. 5232
6. 52,150
7. 83,533
8. 282,268
9. 726,666
10. 7,993,272

page 119

Dividing Whole Numbers

1.   48
2.   53
3.   625
4.   589
5.   63 R7
6.   34 R31
7. 1396
8. 2050 R9

page 120

Operations with Money

1. $3.29
2. $0.94
3. $0.91
4. $60.88
5. $1.56
6. $4.74
7. $50.69
8. $111.11

page 120

Lowest Terms

1. $\frac{1}{3}$
2. $\frac{2}{3}$
3. $\frac{1}{2}$
4. $\frac{3}{4}$
5. $\frac{1}{5}$
6. $\frac{1}{4}$
7. $\frac{2}{3}$
8. $\frac{1}{6}$

page 121

Equivalent Fractions

1. 3
2. 6
3. 6
4. 8
5. 16
6. 2

page 121

Operations with Fractions

1. $\frac{4}{5}$
2. $\frac{5}{8}$
3. $1\frac{8}{15}$
4. $\frac{1}{2}$
5. $\frac{7}{15}$
6. $\frac{7}{30}$
7. $\frac{1}{8}$
8. $\frac{1}{4}$
9. $\frac{2}{5}$

page 132

CROSS NUMBER PUZZLE
A CROSSWORD PUZZLE FOR NUMBERS

			¹2	7	
	²3	0	0		
³1	5			⁴4	2
1				9	
⁵2	⁶5		⁷1		⁸4
	⁹2	0	0		5
			¹⁰1	0	0